MINDFULNESS

Praise for
Mindfulness: The Alchemy of Now...

"*Mindfulness: The Alchemy of Now* is a great contribution to help people seeking to find a real life, simple and full of meaning. Today, when wealth and power govern humans and make them into manipulated pawns, arises Felix Lopez's invitation to rediscover the true humanity inside the 'sapiens.' Tears accompanied the reading of *Mindfulness: The Alchemy of Now,* when I marveled at what we can be, but we are not. Let's start ..."

~Gregorio Riera-Espinoza
Titular Professor of Medicine
Member of the Committee of Scientific Advisors
International Osteoporosis Foundation

"*The Alchemy of Now* finally gives us the meaning of things in life which we never really understood. For me, it was so easy to read that I felt I was having a conversation with Felix himself. FIVE STARS!"

~JP Romano
Music Producer

"Felix shines as a Guru as he explains what it is to be human ... starting from where you are right now to realizing and living your true life's purpose. He prepares you with tools of understanding and wipes away the clutter so you can see clearly what is important, ultimately empowering you to travel mindfully."

~Michael Markus
Yoga Teacher

"*Mindfulness: The Alchemy of Now* is truly a gift to the world. When Felix Lopez spoke to our delegates at the Morocco annual Global Wellness Summit they couldn't get enough of his unique message. Felix's perspective on the topic of mindfulness is indeed beneficial and will help assure that mindfulness practices continue and that peace, joy and a sense of contentment is truly found."

~Susie Ellis
Chairman & CEO, Global Wellness Summit

MINDFULNESS

THE ALCHEMY OF NOW

FELIX LOPEZ

MERRY DISSONANCE PRESS   CASTLE ROCK, COLORADO

Mindfulness: The Alchemy of Now

Published by Merry Dissonance Press, LLC
Castle Rock, CO

FIRST EDITION 2015
Library of Congress Control Number: 2015943962

Lopez, Felix, Author
Mindfulness: The Alchemy of Now

Felix Lopez
ISBN 978-1-939919-19-9
1. Body, Mind & Spirit
2. Spiritualism

Book Design and Cover Design © 2015
Cover Design by Victoria Wolf
Book Design by Andrea Costantine
Editing by Pam Kirby

I dedicate this book to all sentient beings
with ***Mettā***

Mettā is benevolence, friendliness, amity,
friendship, goodwill, kindness.

CONTENTS

A NOTE TO THE READER

MINDFULNESS IS A WAY of living in the present. In the following chapters, you'll begin to understand what it means to truly experience the present moment. The benefits of this life practice are limitless. In entering a state of mind where you are able to be totally present, you can emerge focused on what you're doing and this leads to joy with and in whatever you do. Mindfulness is a way of living more peacefully. Mindfulness allows you to discover and appreciate the hidden treasures that the present moment offers, and to live from the highest level of yourself in each and every moment rather than from your instinctive, basic fears.

This book is intended to give you the opportunity to experience these concepts in ways that will help bring you out of your mind and into your heart, to bring you into conscious living from a place of gratitude, creativity, joy, and peace.

What you'll gain is a deeper sense of love and compassion for yourself, which in turn will allow you to offer more love and compassion to others. Ultimately, you'll develop a more organic relationship with your true nature and others. The journey ahead is an incredible one—offering you a lifetime of unlimited potential.

At the start of every journey, however, is the need to understand where we are currently. We need to understand who we've been and why. We need to look at where we've come from and where we want to go. And we need to consider what is required for the journey ahead, knowing that we may have to pick up more supplies along the way and dispose of some things as we proceed.

As you read this book, I ask that you bring along your sense of curiosity and an attitude of openness. Many of the ideas offered may be completely new to you or they might not have been presented in this way before. You may experience resistance to some concepts or you may have objections to the information. Although the practice of mindfulness is simple, we are a complex species. In our complexity, we often make things more complicated for ourselves than they need to be, and we often create unnecessary obstacles in our growth— even when growth is exactly what we seek. Along with your curiosity and openness, I therefore ask that you suspend judgment as much as possible—of this material and of yourself.

In this book, we will explore the many ways we keep ourselves from being totally present, how mindfulness eludes us in the midst of what we do to survive, to meet our basic needs, and to feel secure in our lives. We'll look at aspects of ourselves that are needed for our survival, yet, when not understood consciously, can actually prevent us from being able to experience joy and peace in our lives. We'll look at the many mechanisms we use that prevent us from staying in the present as well as tools to recognize when and how that happens and what we can do to become more mindful.

As primal beings, we have been programmed to do what is necessary to stay out of harm's way. Those automatic survival mechanisms that are built into us, however, get in the way of living mindfully. Because they've been with us since the beginning of our lives, they aren't easy to recognize and they don't just go away in a matter of minutes or hours. You may, therefore, want to read this book more than once to take in the ideas presented.

One concept that can be very difficult for human beings to comprehend is The Infinite. In speaking about The Infinite, it is difficult to encapsulate something so immense, something beyond our comprehension, into one word or phrase. For the sake of this book and the intention that it is meant to serve all people, no matter your faith, religious background, or philosophical belief, I have chosen to use a symbol to refer to The Infinite. In order not to limit our understanding, throughout this book I will use the infinity symbol (∞) as a reference for what others call God, Buddha Nature, Allah, Higher Consciousness, Jesus, Jehovah, etc. I have mentioned only some of the many names used to refer to The Infinite, but appreciate that there are many more names spoken throughout the world. Knowing that any image, label, or concept is limiting, the infinity symbol seems to best depict that which is beyond all human understanding. Whatever name you use to describe The Infinite, I invite you to insert that name whenever you come to the infinity symbol as you read.

This book is not a religious book. Teachers from some religious traditions are referenced to make the information more understandable, not for the sake of deifying any particular teachers or to convert you to a particular religion or spiritual path. The teachers presented are offered to reinforce your own spiritual beliefs. No matter your spiritual, philosophical, scientific, or religious beliefs, the information presented here is intended to serve you as a human. I offer this information with my deepest love and compassion for every living being.

With Mettā,*

Felix Lopez

---

* Mettā is a Buddhist term that means pure love and compassion that is not attached to any idea, condition, process, outcome, or to anything physical, including people, places, or things. This is love without clinging, without desiring or expecting any results. This is the purest form of love.

THE JOURNEY TO MINDFULNESS

AS WE ALL DISCOVER, life has lots of episodes of sadness, suffering, and difficult moments. Although they may not feel like it, these difficult times are significant moments inviting us to transform the patterns that create suffering in our lives rather than repeat them over and over again, expecting a different outcome. This is often quoted as the definition of insanity, and from my viewpoint, this is exactly what creates the suffering in our lives. In actuality, every single day is an invitation to see what's really going on, to realize how not to repeat the same things over and over, and to find more joy and peace in our lives. Each moment offers us the opportunity to realize that we don't have to suffer. Oftentimes, however, it takes something significant to happen in our lives to get our attention.

In a very difficult and painful time in my life, I realized that I wanted the pain I was experiencing to stop. It was probably the lowest point of depression I've ever experienced in my life. I was enduring tremendous suffering. The only thing I knew was that I wanted what I was feeling to end. I knew I needed to do something different for that to happen, but I didn't know what change was needed, or why or how to create that change.

In my depression, I withdrew. I became isolated. I wanted to deal with my pain alone. I pulled away from everyone and everything I'd been doing. At one point in my suffering I asked myself, "What do you want to do? Do you want to stop living or do you still want to be alive?" I decided that killing myself wasn't an option. I then began a dialogue with myself. "So, if you're going to be here for a while, how do you want this time to be? Can your life be sustainable this way, the way you've been doing it?" The answer was no. I didn't want to live like that anymore. I didn't want to live in so much pain. I didn't want to continue to suffer. I knew the pain was killing me. "So what are you going to do?" I asked. "How are you going to go on from here? Where are you going to go?" I remember saying to myself, "I need my life to be radically different, so now what?"

During that period, I went for the first time to a Buddhist monastery near where I lived. When I saw the monastery, I thought I might find something there, some kind of help and direction. I had been raised with the teachings of Jesus, but I wanted something new. I'd read about Buddhist teachings in the past and remembered that they said a person's pain and suffering would disappear. Because I wanted my physical and mental pain to stop, and because I was searching for a solution, I approached the monastery. It had more to do with wanting to find a way to end my suffering than what I thought or felt about my past relationship with the spiritual teachings of Jesus.

I met a monk in the monastery and told him everything about my situation. For forty-five minutes, and without stopping, I explained my pain and how depressed I was. I remember how he listened to me and at the end he calmly stated, "The problem is that you think too much." At that point I questioned how that was going to help me. I thought that coming to the monastery had been a complete waste of time. He continued, "I'm going to teach you something that's going to help you. It's going to help your mind be a little calmer and a little more relaxed. Believe it or not, that's how you're going to open a space for things to switch a bit. It's called meditation."

I responded, "This doesn't make sense at all." It was not logical to me. As the son of a chemist, I liked logic and reasoning. Yet, all I could think about was how much I wanted to get out of the pain I was in. I desperately needed my suffering to stop, so I decided to give it a try.

In my free time, I began to visit the monastery regularly. The monk assigned chores to me, but I questioned how they were going to help. Little by little, I began to understand that they did help, even though I didn't know why at the time. This monk was introducing me to mindfulness without me even being aware that I was learning it. What I didn't understand at the time was that the chores were an opportunity to focus on something specific and they began to cause a shift within me. As I focused on the chores, I stopped thinking about my life. Even if I didn't like the chore I was doing, that shift in focus stopped my thinking process, which shifted my actions and my emotions. What the monk was doing was providing me with the space to focus on one thing at a time and on the actions I needed to take to perform the chore. He was inviting me to merge myself into the present moment.

As I focused on landscaping, gardening, and potting flowers and plants, I was completely present to those needs, without realizing I was. And working with the flowers and plants, which is very therapeutic, was also healing me. Normally, I would have seen that kind of concentration as a complete waste of time. Yet, when my mind wandered and I thought about my life outside the monastery or about what had happened in the past or what might happen in the future, I began to see how focusing on anything but the present moment made me feel the suffering I'd been struggling with. Those thoughts were the ones that made me feel unnecessary pain—they created suffering within me. When I concentrated on my chores and the actions needed to do them, when I focused on what was happening in the present, I started to feel joyful and experienced moments of peacefulness. It was surprising really. Here I was—someone who'd been involved with a fast-paced life, someone who'd had every material desire—discovering that by focusing and concentrating on simple chores, as well as my behavior and my feelings in that specific moment, I experienced a deep sense of peace.

This monk also made me sit for long periods of time. Imagine someone telling you that they are going to help you by having you sit and then telling you he'll come back in an hour. The only thing I was instructed to do while he was gone was focus on what I could see in front of me. That was it. Imagine! There I sat, feeling the heat and humidity as I looked at what was directly in front of me. Interestingly, though, something began to happen. I started to see more clearly that when I wasn't engaging with my thoughts of the past or future, I was "being" in the present moment, and that experience was giving me a feeling of peace. I began to understand that it wasn't the chores or the details of whatever I was focusing on or doing that brought the peace. It was my relationship with my thoughts and my mental process as I performed the task at hand that began to change my feelings. It was strange, yet the more I felt the effects of focusing on the activities he gave me, the more I learned that whatever I processed as a thought in any particular moment was my reality. I began to see that I had a choice about whether my reality caused me to suffer or made me feel peaceful.

Before spending time in this monastery, I had been logical, always over-thinking things. I was constantly remembering about the past, looking back at what I already knew, or trying to figure out what was going to happen next and why. My mind was constantly working. I lived in my head most of the time. Through the instruction he gave me, the monk taught me how to be aware of my thinking process and relate to my feelings and emotions, which led to observing my behavior and ultimately to becoming an observer of my reality.

After the experience of being completely in the present moment in the monastery, I soon found myself outside a yoga studio. I had never gone to yoga studios before, but because of the openness created by embracing the present moment, I began to pay attention to signals, which led me to this studio. I saw someone inside teaching meditation, and I'd been learning about meditation in the monastery, so I was intrigued and entered.

This visit to a yoga studio led me deeper in my journey and eventually gave me the opportunity to travel to Thailand and India. Through these various experiences and trips, I started to discover that what I was looking for outside myself was actually inside of me—it had been there all along. When I first began to travel, I still thought that what I needed to find was something outside of myself—someone or something that would stop my pain and suffering. In the midst of my pain and suffering, I had believed it wasn't me at all who was responsible for what I was feeling and how I was behaving—I blamed it on other people, on my past, and on my circumstances, believing that all of *that* had caused my suffering.

As I spent more time in different places, I started to see that no matter where I went, I was still capable of repeating the patterns and behaviors that caused me to suffer, but when I embraced the present moment, no matter where I was or who I was with, I felt peace. I realized that it was time for me to stop blaming others for what had happened in my life. I began to understand that when I was in this thinking process of blaming others and focusing on the past or the future instead of engaging in the present moment, I experienced unnecessary pain and suffering, no matter where I was. When I began to see that I was responsible for everything that was happening in my life and engaged in the present moment through the mindfulness practice I'd been learning, the pain started to go away. As a result, I decided it was time to take responsibility for my own life and to acknowledge that I am the creator of my own reality. Through my mindfulness practice of being present in the now, without thinking about the past or the future, I began to connect with what was most important—observing the patterns and focusing on the present moment.

My reality started to change the more I took responsibility for my actions and modified the behaviors that brought me pain. By embracing the present moment and going deeper into my mindfulness practice, the pain and suffering I'd been experiencing stopped. I began to see how my meditation practice was within me no matter where I traveled, and the more time I spent meditating, the more peaceful I felt. I saw that going deeper into my mindfulness practice brought me more peace—it was never something or someone outside of me.

When people ask me what it took for me to change my life, to live in a different way, I tell them that what really helped was being able to understand how I had been living and reacting in the past. I also began to understand my own nature, a big part of which was acknowledging that I had always been a sensitive person. That sensitivity had been there since I was a child. I'd had glimpses in adulthood of tapping into that sensitivity but most of the time, in order to get along and avoid being hurt, I kept it hidden.

What changed my life and made me see things in a different way and find this "thing" that I'd always been looking for was the understanding that in the past I had always been in my mind—living and reacting to the past or worrying about the future. I saw that in the past I had tried to cover up my sensitive nature in order to get along with others, yet covering up my true nature had only caused me unnecessary pain and suffering. In the past, I had blamed people and experiences—things that were outside myself. Through meditation, I realized I had a choice to change the reaction of my mind and to change my mindset. A byproduct of my mindfulness practice was more calmness, more joy, and more peace. I also discovered that it was okay to be a sensitive person—that my sensitive nature was a part of me to embrace. It was okay for me to care for others and to have compassion and empathy for them.

I had been conditioned and taught to listen to my scientific, logical, linear-thinking mind. Through my mindfulness practice, I began to see physiological changes within myself as well as psychological and emotional changes. The more I embraced the present moment, the more my body changed chemically and hormonally. I observed that the neural connections within my mind were becoming stronger and my serotonin levels were more in balance. As my body's chemistry continued to change, I felt healthier and happier. I noticed that whenever I invested my energy in the past or the future, I threw away my energy. I wasted it. Whenever I believed in what I imagined, I saw there was a price to be paid physically and emotionally. Ultimately, I understood that living mindfully means that in each moment I am responsible for my reality, and my actions must come from that understanding. Through my mindfulness practice my life has become radically different, which was what I'd been seeking all along— and it has become so much more joyful and peaceful than I ever imagined possible.

PART ONE

THE HUMAN CONDITION

1

THE HERE AND NOW

MANY PEOPLE SPEAK about mindfulness. It's all over the media. People want to live mindfully and to live in the now, but what people cannot figure out is how to practice it in their day-to-day routines. Everyone is talking about how important mindfulness is, yet most people don't know what to do to keep themselves in the present moment.

As a concept, mindfulness is a very simple practice. It is literally being present by putting all of our attention and energy into the present moment. The concept is simple, but the practice of mindfulness is what is difficult for people, especially in the midst of our very busy, fast-paced lives. And since the majority of society lives in the same survival-based, fast-paced mode of living, where most of us are focused on our basic safety and security, it becomes even more difficult to give our full attention to the present moment—the now—

which in actuality is the only real moment we have. This is what leads to unnecessary pain and suffering in our lives. Our bodies exist in the present moment, yet our minds are constantly traveling between the past and the future.

Why do our minds have such power to take us away from the present? And what is it that pulls us away? With our best intentions, how is it possible for our minds to do things that we are not really giving them permission to do? The answers to these questions lie in the conditioning from the past that can go back generations up to our earliest moments of life. From almost the time we were born, our minds were trained to be in control in order to keep us safe. We developed patterns and habits way back then and we continue to practice those behaviors in order to maintain a sense of security. As a result of those patterns of behavior, we spend most of our time looking at the past in order to ensure that our future will be okay. We live in a state of survival, where our minds control our actions, and this keeps us from being able to live mindfully. Having our minds control our actions is a byproduct of living in this "survival mode" mentality.

Yet, the truth is that it is impossible to get out of the present moment. Whether we like it or not, we are physically where we are, doing what we are doing, at any given moment. We are always in it. The tricky part is to be able to acknowledge that we're in it and to be completely aware of and focused on this present moment.

When I begin to work with someone and explore the concept of mindfulness, I like to ask them to consider whether they can really leave the present moment. After they think about it for a while, they usually respond that they can leave the present by thinking about the past or the future. Then I ask them to consider whether they can *physically leave* the present moment when they think about the past or the future. After a little more contemplation, they respond that they cannot. They might be thinking about the past or the future, but their body is still in exactly the same place it was when their mind went somewhere else.

The only reality we have is the present moment—the here and now—where we are physically. As soon as our mind gets going in anything other than what is right in front of us, as soon as we are not engaging in this present moment, we've left the present mentally. We may begin to worry or anticipate or make plans about whatever the mind is focusing on, whether it's from the past or in anticipation of the future. What we think about might seem important and we might believe it is critical to our safety and security, but it prevents us from experiencing the present moment—the only thing that is actually real. There is no way to concentrate on what is happening in the present moment, which is where our focus needs to be, when our mind goes to the past or future. And, although we may not believe it, being focused on the present moment is the best way to keep ourselves safe.

As primates, human beings' first instinct is to survive and to keep ourselves safe. There are many automatic responses built into the mind of our species to aid us in determining when danger is present and in assessing the steps we need to take to keep us out of harm's way. As humans, however, we are also highly evolved beings. This means that we are not meant to *only* live from our primal instincts or our primal nature of survival. We no longer need to continually live from that "fight or flight" mode of behavior that our earliest ancestors needed in order to survive, yet that mechanism is still built into our minds and our genetics. We are still wired genetically for that kind of automatic reaction to a perceived danger.

As primal beings, our basic built-in survival mechanism is based on seeking pleasure and avoiding pain. The primal mind wants to feel ongoing pleasure. Seeking pleasure can be positive, but it is impossible to sustain a level of constant pleasure. The primal mind also does not like pain, and it seeks to avoid it at all costs. The fact that our primal minds do not like pain is a good thing, because this automatic mechanism acts as a healthy reaction to the possibility of pain. If our mind liked pain, and actually sought out pain, we would be in trouble. What we need to understand, though, is that when our primal mind is allowed to run the show without any system of checks and balances, we can create more problems for ourselves. When that fear-based "fight or flight" mechanism is continually in charge, or when we seek pleasure without any consideration of what is happening right now or what might be the consequences of our behavior, we create the probability of unnecessary pain and suffering in our lives. We also miss the opportunities and experiences that the present moment offers.

As I work with individuals, another concept I invite people to explore is their current level of satisfaction and contentment within their lives. I ask them to look at how joyful and peaceful they are—with their jobs, with their relationships, with their partnerships, with their families. I take it a bit deeper and ask them to consider how satisfied they are with themselves as a human being. I ask them to consider where in their lives they feel a sense of friction—those places where they may be feeling a rub or a sense of uneasiness, discord, or discontent. Basically, in raising these questions, I'm helping them look at where they feel that sense of unhappiness and dissatisfaction within their lives and ultimately within themselves. If there are parts of their lives where they find this friction, that information can help them see where they need to begin their inner exploration. Then, I invite them to identify what is creating the friction and change the reality of it.

Mindfulness has a lot to do with inquiry. The process of exploration and inquiry opens the door to new possibilities. It's like creating new ways of manifesting ourselves as humans. It's learning to discern and make decisions that are for our highest purpose, for our well-being, and for the highest purpose of all humanity. It helps us identify what is important to us and what will lead us to being the healthiest and happiest versions of ourselves. Rather than living reactively we live with awareness of our nature. Mindfulness is the deepest us making decisions rather than listening to our minds—and following our primal instincts.

Most of our suffering, our illnesses, and our physical problems are created when we live only in our instinctive, animalistic vibration and patterning. Even war and killing—the most horrible things we do to each other, to nature, and to other beings—happen as a result of this distortion, this automatic way we normally react.

We *can* change our reality and live more peacefully and joyfully by observing our minds and our instincts that make us act in survival mode. Becoming an observer is key, and that happens as a result of having a mindfulness practice. The practice of mindfulness allows us to move beyond the veils of illusion created by our primal minds—the idea that we must always be ready for impending danger or that we must continually seek pleasure, no matter what. Having a mindfulness practice makes us more aware of those automatic primal responses as well as our psychological patterns and conditioning. It makes us more of a witness to what is happening rather than reacting automatically, almost without any thought before we take action. Becoming a witness, which is strengthened by one's mindfulness practice, creates a buffer where we can observe our minds. This gives us the opportunity to choose how we will respond in a way that serves us rather than to behave reactively.

There are many types of mindfulness practices. They can be physical or mental practices. Tai chi and all types of martial arts require mindfulness. Playing the piano and painting a picture require mindfulness. Chanting is a mindfulness practice. Yoga is a mindfulness practice. Any time we are engaged in an activity where we are completely immersed in the present moment, where we experience no sense of past or future, we are engaged in a mindfulness practice.

When one's mindfulness practice deepens as a result of dedication, commitment, and consistent practice, you find that you are both the participant and the observer. Becoming the observer allows for the creation of the buffer needed before you react. You become the observer and the participant at the same time, and that's the way miracles happen. Time slows down, which gives you the buffer necessary to make decisions as the observer about what you'll do as the participant.

Meditation, one specific mindfulness practice, and the one that has helped me the most in my life, is like going to the gym to train your body. Meditation is a practice that trains your mind so that it becomes stronger in order that you have more control over it. This allows you to live mindfully in the present moment. It leads you to observe yourself and your mind and to create the buffer so you can make more conscious choices. Meditation is a very efficient way of becoming the observer of yourself. And by becoming the observer, you can stop the patterns that lead to pain and suffering in your life.

With the ability to observe, one of the first things you discover is that your automatic survival mode is what produces the mechanisms that create suffering and unnecessary pain in your life. And this relates to every person, of every religion, and at every age—pain and suffering is common to everybody.

2

Pleasure, Pain, Suffering

FROM THE TIME I was a little boy, I always had this feeling that something was missing from my life. Although I had my beautiful family around me and materially I had everything as I grew up, I felt a deep sense of lack. I didn't know why I felt this way, and most of the time I denied my feelings. It was difficult to live with this inner turmoil and this sense of emptiness, so I wanted to get out of my family's house as soon as I could. Thinking I would find what was missing somewhere else, almost immediately after I turned eighteen I left home and began working.

What I hadn't expected was that the sense of lack I'd felt all my life came with me, and I continued to feel that something was missing. I thought I was going to get "it," to feel filled, by making lots of money and acquiring lots of things. Unfortunately, none of this worked. I still felt as if something was missing. So, I had more fun and did more "pleasurable stuff." Still, I felt empty. I was having plenty of experiences and traveling to different places, yet I felt this deep sense of discontentment. I had everything and anything I could imagine, but I was unhappy. Everything I did to increase the pleasure in my life and to decrease the physical pain and the emotional suffering I felt caused more suffering in my life. I didn't begin to understand the vicious cycle I was in until I stepped into that first monastery. That is when I started to see that the peace, joy, and sense of contentment I'd been searching for could not be found outside myself. I needed to look inward.

Pain is not a bad thing; it is an incredible teacher that can awaken a person. Pain is a physical and chemical phenomenon that happens to every living being—and every living being knows about pain. Physical pain is unavoidable. In different vibrations or dimensions—whether an ant, a rabbit, a dog, a plant, or a human being—it is experienced. If we have a body, we are going to experience physical pain—there is no escaping it. Emotional and psychological pain is a part of the human experience as well. Because we are sentient beings, we experience emotions, and those emotions are often accompanied by feelings of pleasure or pain.

Human beings, however, have a strange relationship with pain. We strive to avoid it at all costs. Yet, how many times have you gone through a painful experience and received something beautiful in your life that you were not expecting? How many times have you attempted to avoid a certain situation because you knew it would be painful, only to go through it and think afterwards, "Wow, I am so glad I went through this experience!"? Pain is a teacher that is always available to us. Pain is the way ∞ communicates. When we feel pain or discomfort, it is like ∞ asking us, "What are you doing?" It is an invitation for us to observe, without judgment or blame, what we are doing to create that particular painful situation in our lives.

Usually, these painful experiences are opportunities for awakening. The unhappiness and emptiness I was feeling when I went to that first monastery created an opportunity for me to begin to awaken. At the time it did not feel at all like an opportunity. When we are in the middle of the pain, we don't usually see those moments as the opening for growth and change in our lives. All we know in those moments is that we want the pain to stop. It wasn't until I'd spent some time at the monastery, having the discipline to do what the monk told me to do, that I began to understand I could feel differently. I saw that stopping the pain had everything to do with being completely present to each moment, no matter how seemingly tedious or unimportant, as well as being able to deeply understand the impact of my thoughts on my physical body, my reactions and responses, my relationships, and what I manifest in my life.

In a recent session I had with a group of people dealing with cancer, I expressed that cancer is an awakening process. Many in the group looked at me with shock and surprise on their faces. I know many of them wondered how that could be possible.

I believe that if we can move beyond our fear and judgment of the diseases and conditions that affect people, such as cancer, diabetes, obesity, heart disease, psychological illnesses, etc., and look at them with a sense of love and compassion, we have the opportunity to see these issues in a different way. As with other painful issues in our lives, these conditions are like ∞ sitting with us and asking, "Are you ready? Are we going to do *this* or not?" It is an opportunity to consider why we are alive—to consider our life's purpose and the organic vibration of our true self. It is the opportunity for transformation—for our personal evolution and commitment to our life's path.

This is not a time, however, for judgment and blame. It is not a time to feel bad about what we or others did or didn't do. This is a time when the deepest love and understanding is needed for oneself. This is a time for assessment, not in order to look back and judge, but to look inward and learn how to observe what is happening. This takes the ability to acknowledge our responsibility for our own lives and a commitment to develop a practice where we have the deepest respect for ourselves.

When pain arises, it is therefore an opportunity for understanding—for the acknowledgment and observance of the pain with a sense of neutrality and curiosity. This has happened to me while meditating. Suddenly there is physical pain. Pain can happen because I'm sitting in a certain position. So what happens when I fight the pain and say, "Oh, I am doing this wrong ... I think I need to move"? Responding in this way is how I will miss the point and stop meditating. And guess what happens to that pain that made me move?

It makes me more uncomfortable during the meditation and becomes a very large distraction and is basically the best way for me to stop meditating.

When physical pain arises during my meditation, I have a choice. I can focus on the pain and allow it to stop me from meditating or I can choose to go deeper into my meditation. I can acknowledge the pain and breathe it in. Remember, I am not saying that I *accept* the pain. It is not about accepting the pain. It is about acknowledging the pain and going back to my breathing and exploring what is happening with the pain with a sense of curiosity. And what do you think happens with that pain if I choose to acknowledge it? It becomes less pronounced. It begins to dissipate because in acknowledging the pain rather than fighting it, focusing on it, trying to ignore it, or accepting it, I am not feeding the pain. I am not using my need to control things to interact with the pain.

In the acknowledgment of the pain, there is pure love and understanding that the pain hurts. So imagine if my feet become numb during meditation because they are not getting enough circulation. I may think that my feet are telling me to be careful, but in reality is this true? As soon as I acknowledge the discomfort and tell myself, "It's okay, because a little discomfort is okay. I know that everything will be alright," the pain dissipates.

With acknowledgment of the pain, we create a kind of relaxation, which allows the pain to be released. So whether it's pain caused by circumstances in our lives or physical pain in our bodies, when we can acknowledge the pain with pure love and understanding, as well as a sense of curiosity, that pain diminishes. When we are able to find peace in that relaxation and acknowledge what is happening in our lives or our physical bodies, the pain diminishes.

Imagine, for example, that you are about to receive an injection. Think about what happens when you tense your muscles. Then consider what will happen when you relax the muscles where the shot will be injected. The more you tense, the more the injection will hurt. The more you are able to relax, the less it hurts.

This is the same thing that happens in yoga. When you relax into an uncomfortable pose, it stops feeling so uncomfortable and that leads to more flexibility in your body. In that moment when it hurts, you breathe into the pose. As you breathe, your body is able to expand and relax. The discipline of organically breathing and observing the pain creates a space for you to feel what is real. When you experience physical pain in the midst of a yoga pose, your mind may tell you all kinds of crazy things—even something as silly as the message that your leg is being cut off. Your mind wants you to do something, to take some kind of action, to make the pain stop. In reality, your leg is still attached and will continue to be. So what is real in that moment is that you won't lose your leg—you are simply experiencing pain that doesn't require anything beyond your breath and observation, just as when someone is in meditation. The pain may feel much bigger because of your perception of it, your anticipation of what might happen as a result of the pain, and your engagement in the situation. But in reality, it is just pain.

The moment we take ourselves out of the "organicity" of the situation, our organic rhythm, we fuel the pain—we feed the situation that is causing our pain. As soon as we begin to fight or resist or focus on our pain rather than acknowledge it with love and understanding, we empower and enliven that pain—and that leads us to suffering.

In life, pain is not optional. Suffering, however, is. And there is a difference between the two. Suffering causes a lot of discomfort beyond "present moment" physical and emotional pain. It is my belief that suffering is primarily caused when we become fragmented with time. How exactly does that happen? When we believe the thoughts in our heads.

As human beings we are designed to live in the present moment. The only thing that is real is whatever is happening right now. For instance, as you are reading this book, you may be holding the physical book in your hands, sitting in a chair or on the ground, and allowing the words to enter your mind. Reading this book is the only thing that is real to you at this moment. If your mind is wandering off as you read, maybe to something that happened yesterday or to the errand you need to run later today, you are no longer here in the present. That shift in your focus is what causes you to be fragmented, which leads to suffering. You might be worrying about how soon you need to leave to run that errand. Or you might be feeling the frustration of something that happened yesterday, which is blocking you from absorbing what you are reading right now. Anything other than reading this book that you are holding in your hands is a story. Those stories create images in your mind, but they are not real. They are only images. As long as you go into the past or future through those images and stories, you are disconnected and fragmented in time. And that can lead to suffering.

The possibility of suffering might not seem like much of a problem when you consider the example of reading a book, but what about when it becomes a part of our ongoing daily living? We usually get into this process of going to the past or the future, this break from time, because our mind is trying to avoid pain. In my experience of entering adulthood and believing that I could stop the pain and emptiness I'd felt since childhood, my mind believed that in establishing a career and seeking more of just about everything, I would feel content and fulfilled. Ultimately I found myself suffering physically and emotionally. Had I not been able to see that I needed a radical change, I might have ultimately lost my life.

The mind does not like pain, so it wants to avoid it as much as possible, and at all costs. The mind also tries to gather as much pleasure as possible. This is the way that the mind functions—with a motivation to survive and to experience pleasure. The mind also wants to keep us aware—aware of danger, for example. The way it does that is by making us remember something that happened in the past, usually an experience that was negative.

By taking us to what happened in the past, the mind believes it is going to avoid a repeat of that experience in the present moment. In actuality, this is a huge lie, because the best way for you to avoid pain in the present moment is by staying aware of what is happening right here, right now. The primal mind, however, believes that it is worth it—going away from the present moment. As an evolutionary process, having our mind work in this way was useful. It's entirely possible that this function helped us leave the caves, but this primal mind is rarely necessary in our modern lives. In our modern society, we don't need those primal mechanisms to be as strong or as predominant as they were in our ancestors' lives; however, we frequently use our primal minds as if we still need them—most of the time unconsciously—and this causes us a lot of unnecessary suffering and stress. By staying in the present moment, we can save ourselves from accidents caused by our lack of attention as well as from the experiences of stressful situations caused by our attempts to prevent or avoid circumstances that we believe will cause us pain.

Thinking about the future also causes suffering. It is the other dimension that leads to people's fragmentation. Again, the motivation is to avoid pain or to experience pleasure. It is a means of attempting to control what will happen next, although, in actuality, we have very little control. Yet, we believe we should and do have control over our future—it is an idea that is believed by our society. We place a lot of value in this collective belief and it feels very useful, making us feel as if we can control what will happen in our lives. We think we can maintain complete control—over our finances, our health, our longevity, and more. For instance, think of all the ways we are encouraged to save for the future—for our children's education, for our retirement, for the ability to one day travel and see the world.

The financial element is an especially important one because it touches our basic survival. It goes to our need for security—our ability to meet our basic needs of food, clothing, and shelter—as well as our ability to provide for ourselves and our families. We are told that if we are not taking advantage of all the tools for saving, we are somehow failing and setting ourselves and our families up for future struggle. However, believing we have complete control over our financial future, taking actions to establish that sense of control, and worrying in an effort to remain in control, leads to more suffering and more stress.

The reality is that these beliefs, thinking we can control the future or a particular situation, cause us more stress and can make us sick. They can lead to physical manifestations of illness, whether that illness is mental, physical, or spiritual. Although we want to be as responsible as possible for ourselves and our families, the idea that we can ensure that nothing will ever change causes us to try to hold on so tight to these ideas of how things should be that when reality causes something else to happen, we don't know how to cope. When something doesn't go our way or when the things we thought were going to happen don't occur, we can become devastated, depressed, sick, etc. It is the element of fear underneath that causes stress within us as we try to control for every possibility. Our desire to control things stems from a beautiful intention of survival, of our ego trying to help and protect, but many times the ego crosses the line. We begin to believe that what we imagine is real, which validates that our fears are justified. When we repeat this cycle and overuse it, we suffer. The degree to which we allow our head to believe these thoughts is what leads to an increase in our stress levels.

Being responsible is a beautiful thing, but we have to do it in a way that doesn't cause us to believe all the negative thoughts in our head. Wanting to be responsible for ourselves and others is not bad—again, the intention is beautiful—but we have to be careful about not crossing the line into believing that we can control everything. It can be beneficial to prepare for the future, but then it is important to be able to let go of needing to control what happens as a result of the preparation, and to embrace instead the unexpected that life brings, what is revealed as time goes on, and what we learn in the process.

The discomfort we feel is an invitation. Whether it comes as a result of pain or suffering, it is the opportunity for change. What invites the change comes from our observation and from the information we gather. With that information, then change can happen. When change happens as a result of the invitation, we are peaceful, because it is not forced or coerced or manipulated in any way—it flows from the observation. When we don't allow for the natural evolution of change, when we try to prevent change, or when we attempt to control change, we suffer. That's why suffering has a very deep purpose—it helps us see what we are doing. The discomfort has a meaning.

The discomfort, the stress, is always an invitation to do things a different way. It is an invitation to observe and acknowledge. When we become afraid of the discomfort, we lose our ability to deeply understand. We have very little effect when we are afraid. Oftentimes, we believe we have to be in fear; otherwise, we think we are being irresponsible. In reality, the freaking out doesn't solve anything—it gets us deeper into the mess, deeper into the stress of the situation. In reality what is needed is the ability to relax, to acknowledge what is happening, and to allow for a deeper understanding of what is happening.

Beginning with my experience in the monastery, my teachers helped me see that there was nothing to seek outside myself. My suffering was the opportunity for me to go deeper within myself. The mental and physical suffering I'd endured happened as a result of all I did to seek pleasure and avoid pain. Yet, everything I really needed in order to experience true joy and peace in my life was in each moment. The more present I could be, the deeper was my experience of joy and peace. I needed to stop running or hiding in order to find what I'd always believed was missing from my life. I needed to stop blaming other people or outside circumstances. And I needed to understand my mind and how it worked.

The more deeply we are able to understand how our mind works and why it leads us to the past and future—and the more deeply we are able to have love and compassion for the mind's purpose of avoiding pain and seeking pleasure—the more capable we can become of embracing the present moment and living mindfully. That begins with understanding some of the conditioning and mechanisms at play within us.

3

PERFECTIONISM

AS PART OF OUR HUMAN conditioning, we suffer in our attempts to strive for perfection. We strive to have the perfect family, to have the perfect children, to be the perfect parent, and to experience the perfect moment. It's all illusion, though, just as much as our belief that someone else's life is perfect and ours isn't. It's our imagination that makes us see someone else as having the perfect anything. When we compare ourselves to others, to what is around us, or to what has happened in the past, what we are really doing is providing validation that we are not good enough. This is our ego at work.

When you consider being a "perfect parent," for instance, what is a perfect parent really? A parent who is ready for whatever happens. A parent who is present to whatever is happening. A parent who does the best they can in every moment. There will be beautiful times with our children, and there will be difficult times with them. Yet, every moment is perfect. Our children are constantly changing—and they are neither good nor bad. This is the beautiful reality of what is, so it's up to us to create harmony with that. No negotiations, no bargaining, no wishing, no going back, and no looking forward.

Everything changes. Period. And that is perfection. There is perfection in every moment—what was, what is, and what will be. It is up to us to create something beautiful with that movement—that is what perfection is for each of us. Perfection is the ability to create harmonious interaction with that movement rather than seek something beyond the here and now or outside ourselves.

When we are content with each moment, when we experience each moment as perfect, the ego struggles to feel its aliveness. The ego wants us to believe that we or the moment are not enough so that we will keep moving and keep going. The ego feels desperate when it doesn't feel needed anymore. What do we have to give the ego when that happens? The ego has to realize that the concept of achieving perfection is an illusion—that it is not reality. It has to acknowledge that our beliefs are just thoughts. The thought of a banana will not take your hunger away. The thought is useful because you can use your nose to search for a banana, but the thought of the banana will not save you. Thoughts will only give you the direction towards what is true.

We are wired to believe that we're born messed up. "Original sin" is a perfect example of the messaging that many people receive from the very beginning of their lives. In certain religions, we are told that we were born sinners. We are taught to believe the notion that there is something inherently wrong with us. The implication is that we come into the world with a mark and that our life's purpose is to remove that mark and to learn not to give into our natural tendencies to sin.

It feels to me that these religious institutions don't want people to have a good relationship with their instinct or their true nature. The intention behind what is communicated is to make people feel as if their instincts are a bad thing and their true nature is wrong. By making people feel this way, the institutions can then make people believe they need the institution in order to be saved—that without the institution they will remain inadequate, worthless, and that they will never be okay.

In reality, our instincts are not bad, and neither is our true nature. What creates suffering for us is when we use our instincts in ways that we aren't conscious about, often unconsciously denying or pushing away our instincts and our true nature. What we need to focus on is what is not working well in any particular moment—not that we are BAD. There are times in our lives when our instincts work well for us. This is the part that can become confusing, because we usually look at what we've done in terms of right or wrong rather than what we might have needed to do in order to survive. Oftentimes, our instincts help us survive and cope with situations in our lives. Sometimes what we do is not a healthy coping mechanism, but at those times it may be the only thing we can do to survive.

Let's say, for instance, that someone drinks to cope with the psychological effects of an abusive relationship. Maybe the person drinks a lot. If we look at that person in terms of what is bad or good, or right or wrong, we might say the person is bad and wrong for what they are doing—drinking too much and being drunk more than they are sober is not a good thing. But in that person's particular circumstances it might be the healthiest way for them to cope—and maybe the only way for the person to survive the situation. Their actions might be the most perfect way for them to continue. Maybe one day, however, the person wakes up and realizes they need to stay sober so they can pull themselves together and get out of the relationship. They realize that what they've been doing no longer serves them and that to save their life, they must leave. That is perfection as well, because they are taking a new and different action for their ongoing survival. What the person did prior to this moment of clarity was not right or wrong or good or bad—it was their instinct for survival that kept them going.

We look at perfection in terms of judgment—of what appears right or wrong or good or bad. We also have this idea that perfection is something static—that once we achieve it we need to stay "there." Perfection, if you think about the most important quality of ∞, is not static. ∞ *is always changing.* ∞ is change itself. Nature is change itself. The perfection of nature is that it is always changing. Perfection is not something to reach for and achieve—it is not a place that we get to and then it doesn't move anymore and everything is going to be perfect. Your ego, though, sees it differently. Your ego wants perfection to look a certain way, and then when you get to that point, it wants to hold that "perfection" and not allow anything to change. The ego wants to keep things the same. But the nature of life is that this is not possible.

Perfection is not an end goal. Perfection is the allowance of change to happen. For instance, what is perfection for a professional racecar driver? A good racecar driver drives "perfectly," but what does this look like? To start with, racecar drivers have developed driving skills that are second nature to them. And that means that they are really good at managing whatever changes occur on the track—whether that's due to weather, the positions of the other drivers, or some other external variable. The racecar driver has the instinct to react to change quickly, to make fast responses to the conditions on the track, and therefore to change as necessary. This ability to change has everything to do with flexibility. So, it's flexibility that allows a racecar driver to drive perfectly. If you take a racecar driver to a different racetrack, after the driver goes around a few times they know exactly what to do to handle the new track. Racecar drivers adapt to the new setting and to the new circumstances. It's this flexibility—this ability to adapt to whatever is different—that makes what they do so perfect. It's what makes the driver a champion. When they go to a track in another country or region, they are able to adapt to the changes in humidity, temperature, elevation, and every other condition they encounter. They use what they know and apply it to the new conditions. They are able to change and be flexible, and they are "perfect" in their ability, no matter what changes are required.

You can apply this same idea to a musician. The rhythm can change, the mood can be different, the tone might change—yet the musician can still perform the music, acknowledging the change and adapting to it. A singer can even sing with a cold—adjusting to a lower range. The outcome can be different but the music will still be beautiful. That's why when you hear a performance live it is always a little different than when you heard it before—whether it was another live performance or a recording. Perfection is being able to adapt— but it is still perfection. Different but still perfect. If you think you can only sing it one way in order to be perfect, that's the distortion.

We may feel that going in the direction of perfection is a beautiful thing, but we're actually setting ourselves up for suffering. Because constantly striving to reach some perceived level of perfection puts a person into a living hell. Yes, it's a beautiful thing that we want to be better people—to be more loving, more productive, more spiritual—and to try to be the best we can at the best level possible. But to live our lives thinking that we'll be happy when we get to that perfection is the hell, because it will never be enough.

When a person feels that they must become perfect and they keep striving for that perfection, they get caught in a cycle of feeling that what they're doing is never enough. They live with a sense that if they don't get there, to some perceived finish line, they're not good enough, which can lead them to give up. And that leads to an ultimate feeling of worthlessness.

Perfection is like the mercury in a thermometer. Do you remember breaking a glass thermometer and then trying to pick up the mercury—to grab the little balls with your fingers? It's impossible to pick up those pieces of mercury. You could spend years trying to pick them up but you never will. Perfection moves like that. You can never grab perfection because it is evolution in process. In every moment that we are trying to achieve perfection, evolution is happening. Perfection is always changing—it's ∞. Always changing—always moving.

Let me give you an example of perfection in motion. So far there is nothing better than a CD for music playback, but in a few years the CD will be replaced technologically with something else—something that will improve the quality of the sound and provide other enhancements. Do you remember when record albums were replaced by CDs and we couldn't believe it? Think of each recording technology that we've evolved through, including the eight-track tape and the cassette tape. Remember how with each new invention we exclaimed "Wow!"? We weren't looking for anything better because with each new sound playback device we couldn't imagine anything more. Maybe something someday will be smaller than an iPod and higher quality than a CD, and the idea of that is a beautiful thing. Each new thing that evolves is beautiful. Yet, when you consider a record album today, can you see how it is still an amazing product? It is still perfection. The record album was not a failure or a mistake, and neither was the cassette tape. It would have been impossible to have the knowledge and creation of the CD if we hadn't first experienced the invention of the record album or the cassette.

Look at how the computer has evolved and continues to be transformed. Is the magnetic card of the past invaluable because of the way computers have evolved? It is a mistake to see any of what came before as an error or waste of time.

And that's the same with us. Whatever we've lived through is part of our evolution. There is nothing that was a mistake or a waste of time in our lives. We were perfect then—we are perfect now. We have simply evolved.

4

DEFENSE MECHANISMS

FROM THE TIME of my earliest memories, I couldn't understand the adults in my life. I honestly thought they were a little crazy. I couldn't grasp why these adults seemed to be ruining their lives when, from my perspective, life seemed to be so enjoyable. It didn't make sense to me why these older people only focused on the problems in their lives when my life was filled with so many fun and beautiful moments. At that young age, it seemed that life itself was beautiful and was meant to be enjoyed.

The fact that very young children see things differently than those who are older is an issue of linguistics (and the difference between humans and other animals). Let me show you how this happens.

Let's take the example of a cat. When we were very little we didn't know how to write the word "cat" or identify a cat with the word "cat." For us at that very young age, "cat" was a beautiful thing. The concept was not important; it was the animal itself and the experience of being in front of the animal that was the beautiful thing. We didn't need to know that the cat was a cat—we didn't need to know about any name or classification or information. We just knew that we found the experience of the cat to be beautiful.

In time, in order to communicate and to relate to the other people in our lives, we began to classify it as a cat. In the most basic sense, we used this classification in order to survive.

But by classifying and naming it, we lost our connection to the essence of the cat—a cat no longer was this incredible being in front of us. It became more of a mental object. It became a word that contained a lot of information—all the explanations for what this word meant. In reality, the word "cat" had nothing to do with the animal anymore. Intellectually, a cat became a series of attributes. It was an animal that was different from a dog. It usually was a pet to us or to someone we knew. It might have been a stray, living out on the street. It had a specific color and size. It was a certain gender, and maybe we knew its age. The cat became this thing that represented a lot of very specific details that distinguished it from all other "things." It had certain behaviors and characteristics. Maybe someone we knew had been scratched by a cat and that became part of the information we understood about "cat." With all the information imposed on us, however, cat lost its beingness. Cat was no longer what it had been to us in the beginning. It became a word "cat" along with all the explanations for what this word meant.

In reality, the word cat has nothing to do with the animal. The cat doesn't even know that it is called cat. It has no idea that it is a cat. The word becomes a way for us to identify the cat, to differentiate it, and to talk about it—to communicate about it. In time, our whole community forces us to believe that the real concept of cat is the word "cat" more than the essence of the cat. We begin to put a lot of emphasis on the concepts we've come to associate with the word "cat," and in the process we lose our connection to this being that we understood experientially in the beginning.

Before you knew who you were because of the name you were given at birth, you experienced yourself as spirit that nourished you with everything you were seeing, hearing, feeling, tasting, and more—literally in the beginning you were ∞ having the experience of being ∞. This was how you experienced yourself as a baby.

In time, society forced you to believe that you were your name, and that you were the concepts that went along with your name. That may sound like it's not important or significant, but I think this is where everything really begins. It is the trigger for trouble. No longer being ∞ experiencing the sensations of living, with your name comes the concept that you are a person who does certain things and acts in certain ways—you talk a certain way, you have certain beliefs, and you behave in certain ways. So the concepts of who you are become merged with all these ideas of your label—your name.

But if you think about it, your name is not so real. It is a concept. People may believe this concept, but in reality the essence of you is something else. Although you are encouraged to be the concept of you, the essence of you is something quite different. You are not just your name and what is attached to that name. You can change, you can evolve—you can become something and someone completely different. You do not have to stay as the YOU that you've been in the past. Your essence can evolve.

Yet, we tend to believe more in the concepts than in the reality. We have these concepts in our head, so when the reality and the concept are not the same it gets confusing. For instance, I can go off to Europe and learn to play soccer. In the process of becoming a skilled soccer player, I am undergoing a transformation and having this beautiful experience of "becoming" something new—something different. Before I left, I might not have been someone who played any kind of sport. So when I return home I may encounter a prior acquaintance who has certain beliefs about who I was prior to the time I lived in Europe. It's possible they won't be able to see who I've become. It's possible they may not be able to believe that I am now a skilled soccer player, maybe even a player who is being sought after to play professionally. It may be extremely difficult, or even impossible, for them to reconcile their concept of who I was with the person who now stands before them. This past acquaintance may come to the conclusion that I'm making the whole thing up.

This example might sound a little silly, but think about it for a moment. When you make radical changes in your life, people may not believe it's still you because their idea of you—their concept of you previously—no longer matches with the reality of you. When the reality of you is not the same as their concept they have to create a story. They have to come up with some explanation to explain what's happened in order to make sense of what is different. So in their mind you might have become someone who lies, or is sick, or is mentally unbalanced—or something else. In reality, in the core of reality, it is a whole bunch of ideas, of beliefs, that are created based on what they knew from the past.

The idea of becoming a soccer player seems benign, but what about when it's something more significant? Let's say you grew up in a family that drank wine at dinner—even the children were given wine. They loved to have wine with their meal, and so did you as you grew up. As you got older, though, you were exposed to other ways of living. In the process, you decided to no longer drink wine. You now do not drink wine under any circumstance. When you return home for a special occasion and your family serves wine to you, because they hold a concept of you as someone who drinks it, you politely decline. Imagine how your family may react to this information. The YOU who is now in front of them does not match the YOU they knew. The reality of you does not match their concept of you. So, again, they may make up a story in order to reconcile this incongruence.

In Hinduism they call the state we live in "maya"—they say we live in a dream world. Living in this dream world, when we wake up each morning we go straight to all these concepts and ideas of who we and others are. Yet all of it is a dream. It is like being in a dream state where we believe these concepts of ourselves and others, even though the concepts are not the reality.

In reality, we just are, and every day we can be whatever we *are* that day. Each day, you are free to be whatever you are. If you don't believe in the concepts, you're free to be *anything* each and every day—you are free to be whoever you want to be! You don't have to be what you were yesterday, and you don't have to be what others believe you to be. Tomorrow you can be a totally different person, too, even though yesterday you were something else. For instance, yesterday you might have been sick or suffering with a medical condition, but to-morrow you can be a completely healthy person. Yesterday you may have drunk wine, but tomorrow you can be someone who doesn't drink alcohol.

Just as our attributes can change from day to day, our beliefs are also always changing, so it would be crazy to believe that our beliefs remain true. When we believe that *what we believe* is true we get into pain. When we believe our thoughts, we suffer.

It is very important to understand the significance of our thoughts and the concepts we get locked into, because they help us understand defense mechanisms and how they work. Defense mechanisms are completely logical. They make sense because they protect us. But it's extremely important to see how these defense mechanisms are created, how they work, and how they can lead to suffering.

As soon as we are born, defense mechanisms are formed within us. From the very beginning of our lives, and without our intentional participation, these defense mechanisms be-come a part of us. They get created and we use them—all automatically, without any conscious thought. They begin to be created through our conditioning—through our family's culture, values, and beliefs—and they are communicated to us most especially through language. Just like our name and the concepts that go with our name, defense mechanisms are imposed on us by our families, by society, through our upbringing, through religious and educational institutions. These defense mechanisms are imposed on us without our permission or consent in the same way our name and the concepts of who we are have labeled us in certain ways. And just like we may never give a second thought to the fact that our name doesn't really depict the real us, we all have built-in defense mechanisms that we don't even realize we possess and activate. When we are young, our defense mechanisms may serve us well—keeping us safe and out of harm's way. As we grow older, however, just like the concept of "us" can begin not to fit the reality of who we are, our defense mechanisms can begin to cause more difficulties in our lives than help.

For example, let's say that a person realizes when they are young that they are homosexual, but because of their family's belief system and values they cannot disclose this information. The individual might even carry this into their adult life by denying their sexual orientation. They may even eventually marry someone of the opposite sex to conform to their family's beliefs and keep their family happy. This defense mechanism has been put in place to keep everyone safe. At some point, however, the individual may become so miserable that they can no longer deny their sexuality.

We also develop defense mechanisms through our life experiences, and using an example, I'm going to show you how this works. Imagine that in the past you hurt me. Long ago, you made me suffer. As a result of what happened back then, I developed a concept of you that you are the person who hurts me. In my ego mind, that's a reality—I can even prove to you that you hurt me before. But as we saw in the example of becoming a soccer player, that concept I have of you is a thought in my head because of something that happened in the past. It is not based on what may be the reality today.

So, what if you realized you hurt me and you became willing to change your ways and to become a new person for me because you love me? Let's say you make that decision and then one day you come back to me and say, "Felix, I am here to say hello. I am a new person." If I believe more in my concept of you based on the past than your intention or who you've become, I'm going to suffer. I can guarantee that I'm going to make you suffer as well. So if I believe the concept of you—and that you could never change—those concepts multiply and amplify.

What gets multiplied and amplified is what makes us and others suffer. Those concepts are how we burn ourselves, how we traumatize others, how we lose opportunities, and how we get completely confused.

This is one way that defense mechanisms are formed and this is what is created when we use them in the wrong way. Instead of me being able to see the new you, I see the horrible person who mistreated me, and based on my concept of you, I believe that behavior will be repeated again. There was a time when I needed to defend myself, but how will you feel if I continue to react that same way, as if you haven't changed?

When you put yourself out there as this new version of you, but I continue to react as I reacted to you in the past, you may get to the point where you no longer try to make me see the new you. You're now hurting because in order to change it took a lot of energy and clarity—and a lot of truth. But because you are now hurting, you might decide to go back to how you were before, or at least stop trying to make further transformation within yourself. If I remain afraid of getting hurt again and keep the concept of you that used to hurt me in order to protect myself, you may get to the point where you stop your personal evolution because it hasn't worked. So now we are both hurting.

When we believe that our beliefs are truth we suffer. We believe our thoughts rather than what IS in the moment. Because we believe our thoughts we block reality—we keep ourselves from seeing the NOW. We react based on the past or what we believed about someone from the past. We are afraid of getting hurt again or afraid of the person being different from our concept of them, so we hang on tight to the concept of who they were or what happened previously without checking to see if anything has changed, without allowing for theirs and our own evolution.

We repeat the defensive responses we are unconscious about. This is a healthy mind doing what the mind does best. If I deeply understand this with my heart, I understand that there is no way *not* to remember the past experience. There is also no way *not* to react automatically based on my earliest conditioning. With love and compassion, I can understand that I am going to feel the past experience—I am going to feel the adrenaline, along with the other stress hormones, that come up with any reminder of a past experience.

We will remember past experiences, and we will feel the pain of the past. We will also have automatic "go to" responses. However, we want to be able not to react or believe based on our past conditioning. So that's where the buffer comes in—what I refer to as "the gates of heaven." When we can learn to acknowledge what is happening with love and compassion and value what our memories or beliefs are trying to tell us, it is a very beautiful thing. It is our ego mind trying to protect us. But being able to acknowledge rather than immediately react creates a completely different outcome. It means we have a choice as to whether or not we or anyone else suffers. By acknowledging rather than reacting we allow ourselves to see and focus on what's real NOW rather than focusing on what we believe based on the past.

Every time we believe our thoughts we burn ourselves. The concept is never reality; the concept is always a concept. It is an illusion. Reality is only what is happening right now in the present. We know that the body doesn't know what's real and just follows thoughts, so we have to look beyond what we may be feeling in our body. We can acknowledge the physical sensations we're feeling, but once again, we need to allow ourselves to focus on what is happening NOW rather than react to what happened in the past. We also have to become conscious of the thoughts we tell ourselves. Once more, that's where the buffer comes in. The more we can allow the space to see what is really the truth now, the less we will suffer.

When we can understand with love and compassion that our past responses were a reaction because we were in pain, then we can understand that every moment is a new moment and doesn't have to play out the way it did in the past. Every moment is a NEW MOMENT. Every moment is CHANG-ING. Every moment is DIFFERENT. Every moment is EVOLVING. And that is the way ∞ likes it—evolution in every moment. The pain and the hurt are based on the past. The moment we allow the space to see the reality of NOW, truth manifests through us, and that is holy and sacred—allowing for the new, allowing for the expression of ∞.

PART TWO

WHAT IS REAL?

5

THE ROLE OF TRUTH

LET'S START WITH what is. The truth is. The truth exists—it was, it is, and it always will be. The truth always reveals itself. In my understanding, the truth is what many religions refer to as "God's will." The truth is what has happened. For me, reality is absolutely connected with ∞. Reality is truth, and truth is ∞. The truth is what is happening, whether we believe in it or not. Whether we agree with it or not, the truth happens. It is always happening—it is infinite. The truth is something that is not going to stop anytime soon. It continues, whether we acknowledge it or not.

Life happens. The truth is life itself. Some of it we like and some of it we dislike. There are parts of the truth that can freak us out at times. There are no explanations that come with the truth. The truth just is. The truth happens whether we understand it or not. We cannot stop the truth. Our understanding is not a requirement for truth to exist. Sometimes we understand the truth and sometimes we do not.

The truth is something we cannot judge—it is not possible. We may try, and most of us do it a lot, but the truth is much bigger than any judgment. There is no right or wrong to the truth—the truth simply is. There are no mistakes to the truth. The truth does not mean that everything will be okay or that there will always be a "happily ever after." Again, the truth just is what it is—no good or bad, no better or worse.

As humans we want to make sense of everything. Our linear-thinking minds want and need that sense of order—of one thing following another, of one event leading to the next. So, when faced with a truth, we want to assign meaning and significance and judgment to what we see and experience. With our mind, we want to interpret the truth and we want to put it into some kind of context. We assign our perceptions to the truth. *Maybe the tsunami happened to punish people. Maybe she won the lotto because she is a good person; maybe he didn't get the raise because he didn't deserve it.* We attach meanings to the truths that confront us in order to comfort ourselves.

When we are able to observe the truth with an open heart, however, we have a very different experience of it. When confronted with a truth that doesn't make sense—for instance, an earthquake that levels a city—if we come from our heart, we can be open enough to acknowledge the truth as reality. We are able to sit with the truth, even when it is painful. Sometimes, we come to understand the deeper meaning of the truth and sometimes there is no basis of understanding. Natural disasters can usually be understood with the help of science. However, a child being molested is beyond most people's understanding. As difficult as it may be to do, our open heart is what allows us to ultimately acknowledge the truth.

Think about your own life. Have you ever found yourself hating the truth, being in complete disagreement with the reality of a situation? And then times goes by and one day you reflect back and see the blessing of that past situation? Over and over, I have had that experience in my own life. Those experiences are an invitation to stay open and see what the truth reveals, because the reasons that things happen are usually bigger than what I can see in a single moment.

Allowing for the space of what may be later revealed takes faith. Faith is also what is necessary when there is no revelation of the deeper meaning, because sometimes what is revealed is so far removed from us that we cannot see it—we may never be able to see it. We may not like the truth of a situation either; again, we don't have to like it. What is required is to understand that there may be a reason deeper than what we can comprehend in this moment. We can be ignorant about the dynamics at play and yet accept the truth of the present moment. That acceptance creates trust. With faith, we can accept the truth of the present reality so completely that we are able to trust it.

With faith, an open heart, trust, and deep understanding we can create incredible flexibility within ourselves to accept what is. Of course, because we are human beings who possess minds, this can be a very difficult practice. Especially when our lives appear to be in danger, when there seems to be a risk to our survival. In the case of the tsunami, let's say we are on an island and we know there is a tsunami coming. Our minds will try to control the truth of the situation, and this gets us into a place of friction within ourselves. We may try to convince ourselves that this is not actually happening, that the weather people got it wrong.

Once we acknowledge the truth of the situation, that the tsunami is actually coming, we are faced with the option of embracing what is about to occur. That ability to embrace what is happening does not mean that we don't take some kind of action. There is a huge difference between apathy—just sitting down on the beach and waiting for the wave to come—and embracing what is.

Let me give you another example to demonstrate the difference. Suppose you get the sense that you may be fired from your job. You may decide to go home, sit on the sofa, and watch TV, believing everything happens for a reason and trusting that there is a bigger plan at play. You may decide to sit there and pray for the next job to come if you do lose this one, believing that ∞ will provide. Unfortunately, this is a big misunderstanding because there is not only an external deal going on; there is an internal one as well. You have a responsibility in what happens next. So, the question becomes, "What do I need to do, what is my part, and what needs to be left to ∞?" We need our highest level of consciousness—our open heart, our faith, our trust, our deep understanding, our love and compassion—to allow information to come in at the only moment that exists, which is the present moment. We need to allow that level of consciousness to guide our actions. Those actions, because they come from our deepest self, will be extremely powerful. Maybe it means going home and sending out resumes to other companies, maybe it means figuring out if you need to do something to correct the reason for possibly getting fired. Our open heart will guide our actions.

In the case of the tsunami, maybe we'll decide to prepare as much as possible to save ourselves. Maybe we'll go to the highest ground we can possibly find. Maybe we'll buy a plane ticket to leave. Maybe we'll go to some underground bunker. Maybe we'll get involved with rallying as many people together as we can to lead ourselves to safety. Again, our highest level of consciousness will guide our actions. These actions all demonstrate acknowledgment of the truth—what is happening outwardly in the present—while looking inward to see how best to address it.

When confronted with a situation where the outcome is not clear, yet there is a threat of some sort, the ego mind wants to jump in. It sends you certain messages—mainly to worry—by automatically taking you to the past or future. But what might happen if you keep yourself completely present, in total peace, and consider what you need to do in the present moment? This is the invitation! Rather than getting wrapped up in the illusion of what is going to happen in the future or what happened in the past, you are invited to stay completely present to what is happening right now.

Our ego mind wants to take us into fear. And, if we give into it, that fear will block the possibility of our highest self being able to act. It also blocks our ability to connect with ∞, the potential for the manifestation of the "Highest Truth." It limits the potential for the truth to be revealed. If the ego mind is in control, we limit the potential outcome. With fear, there are two ways we usually respond. We either become apathetic or convince ourselves that we have complete control.

When we become apathetic, we are unable to act. Rather than a surrendering, an embracing of what is happening in the present moment, we check out. We may trick ourselves into thinking that what we are doing is surrendering to what is, but in actuality, because we are removing ourselves and our personal responsibility from the equation, we are allowing fear to control us. Apathy is like freezing in place.

The other way fear shows up is that we convince ourselves we have complete control of the situation; maybe even that we are invincible. Yet underneath what our ego mind is relaying is complete fear. We really don't believe we are completely in control. We really don't believe we can stop our boss from firing us any more than we can stop the tsunami from reaching shore.

What all the teachings of the greatest teachers invite us to do is live in the truth. They invite us to be love. To be understanding. To be wisdom. To be infinite. To allow the truth, ∞, to move through us and come out through our actions. We are asked to be infinite power. We are invited to be Buddha, to be Jesus, to be Mohammed in action, with total faith and trust, with an open heart, with deep understanding. Living in the truth in this way brings magic. It is magic. It is not us. It is something way more powerful than you or me.

You know you are not denying the truth when you are not suffering. You know that you are allowing the truth to move through you, you know you are not trying to control the truth, when you feel a deep sense of peace and joy. There is no resistance. Although your ego mind may be uncomfortable and may not like the truth, you are able to allow enough space within for your highest level of consciousness to come through, for you to be in action. There is a sense of peace that accompanies your actions because you know you are doing the best you can, you are taking responsibility for your part without trying to control the truth in any way.

When our actions come from our heart, from ∞, we create the potential for quantum* reaction—for quantum manifestation. And how beautiful is that? When we are no longer acting from our heads, when our actions are done without expectation, we allow for the highest level of truth to reveal itself. Only the highest good can happen from that. We don't know how things will turn out, but we have faith and trust that right actions lead to right results. The highest version of ourselves is at play rather than the small "us" based in fear, and that changes everything—that changes reality. That allows for the highest version of truth to occur.

Though most of us often allow our ego minds to run things, which causes tremendous suffering, through practice we each have the potential to react in a way that reveals this higher truth.

---

* Quantum *adj*: sudden and significant

6

THE BIGGEST LIE

BELIEVING THAT OUR MIND or someone else's mind speaks the truth is the biggest lie we can tell ourselves. Our mind is constantly trying to make sense out of what we don't know. It goes to something that occurred in the past but is not happening right now or something that will happen in the future based on previous experiences. This causes us to live in a fragmented state.

It's so important to remember that even if things are not happening right now, we can feel them as if they are. When we access something that happened in the past through the folders that are in our heads, we feel the effects of the event as if it is happening in the present moment. Most likely, we are then not able to pay attention to what is actually happening right now, which is the best way for us to make a mistake. It could be a car accident or a missed exit on the road. It could be losing my footing on the stairs or sidewalk. Or it could be my inability to hear what a friend or client is telling me in a face-to-face conversation. And that mistake, no matter how big or small, is going to lead to a result in the future—most likely an undesirable one. When I am not focused on the present moment because I have been pulled back into the past, it can mess up the future, since I am not doing what is required in the present. These are examples of fragmentation.

Looking to the future can also cause us to make mistakes in the present. We usually look to the future because we are trying to avoid something that we worry will happen, but just like when we look back, we get fragmented. This can cause more problems in the present and once again impact our future.

Let me give an example of what can happen when we look to the past. If I am attracted to someone, I need to understand that my mind is going to remember the past. Let's say I had a bad experience with a previous relationship. That does not mean I will have a bad experience with the new person, but automatically my mind is going to take me to the bad experience to make me aware. My mind is going to give me a big "BE CAREFUL" warning. It will continue to provide that message, "Be careful … be careful … remember what happened before."

The fact that my mind provides this message is a good thing. It can actually be very positive. The problem begins if I believe that warning signal as something that is true in the present. That is the best way for me to ruin a new relationship, because most likely this new person has nothing to do with the previous one. But when I begin to identify this new person as the one from the past, I begin to repeat my patterns related to that past relationship—which will guarantee that the new relationship fails.

In order to avoid such an outcome, it is necessary for me to bring in my deepest intuition through my heart. Since my mind is looking and evaluating and trying to make sense of what is happening right now based on what happened before, I need to acknowledge the signal and thank my mind for bringing up the folder filled with memories of the previous relationship. Rather than act from an instinctive level, however, I need to go to a conscious level—the conscious part of me that is telling me to remember the pain I experienced in the past, which is good for me to remember because it's good information. But I don't stop there. I then bring myself to the present moment, which is the only moment that is real, and acknowledge what is happening right now. I can see that what is happening in my mind is based in fear and insecurity created in the past. It is not real in the present moment. I then acknowledge that the past pain is not real now. It is my mind remembering my previous experience. I can feel everything I felt when the pain occurred. It is a mental image, though, that has no value in the present moment other than to remind me not to make the same mistake again. That is the only value the past provides. It's a beautiful practice when I can acknowledge the signal and then say to myself, "I understand this is just an image of my mind. This is not real. I am back now. Thank you."

We ruin many things in our lives—many potential opportunities, experiences, and relationships—by believing a past event is happening right now and acting from that belief rather than the very real present moment. I am not suggesting that we ever deny what happened previously. It does not mean that we should not look at the past or recall how we felt back then. It does not mean that we should deny our minds or try to convince our minds not to say anything (which is impossible to do). It *does* mean that we allow our minds to provide us with information, acknowledge that information, and then look at the present to determine what is real and what is optimal NOW. It's incredible how much suffering human beings experience by either allowing the mind to control our actions or trying as hard as we can to deny our minds. Both cause us to suffer.

Another aspect of the biggest lie we believe comes as a result of our conditioning. Much of that conditioning comes from our religious, cultural, and familial upbringing. I am not suggesting that anyone turn away from their religion, culture, or families; however, I do believe it is important to understand the conditioning that was imposed upon us (and I include myself in this because I too was raised in a religious tradition that impacted how I viewed myself and the world around me).

Let me provide another example. Let's say that a young woman has a sister and every time the she speaks to her sister the she feels sick. The conversations are unhealthy, so every time they interact with each other she feels nauseous afterwards. Yet, it is a tradition in her family to get together every weekend with her entire family for dinner. The young woman goes every weekend because that's what is expected of her. You see, that weekly interaction is based on an instinct to survive. Yet, this need to attend a weekly family event is a lie as well. Through the conditioning she has received, she believes that she must attend and that if she continues to attend, eventually she and her sister will become closer. Based on past conditioning, she believes that continuing to try to build a healthy relationship with her sister is good. The young woman believes she is becoming a stronger, better person as a result of trying. So she continues to try … and she tries and tries and tries. Then maybe she goes to speak to an advisor, maybe it is someone in her family's church. She comes away believing that she must continue to try because maybe she's just not doing enough to make things better. Maybe the message she receives makes her think she's not good enough, not patient enough, not attentive enough. And that is how we become physically and mentally sick. We keep trying to survive situations that would be better for us to distance ourselves from.

Most of us have a difficult time letting go of people and situations when our conditioning has taught us to persevere. We're told that no matter what, we must try. We're told it is the right thing to do and that we are being good people when we do so. We're told we must be there for our families or communities or organizations *no matter what*. We're told we must endure—wanting to be a good human being, it is our duty to do so. And believing the message that in order to be good we must keep trying, we strive to do the right thing. It becomes a part of what we do to survive. Most of the time, we are not able to recognize the harm that it is doing to us. We think that today will be different than yesterday, even though we have no indication that that possibility even exists.

I am not suggesting in this example that the young woman shouldn't go and create a beautiful relationship with her sister. I am not saying that it isn't possible for her to have a good relationship. What I am questioning is how we go about it. I believe that is where the problem begins. In this example, the young woman must ask herself whether or not she is respecting herself. In going every weekend and having the same outcome, is she taking care of herself and her needs? Is she respecting herself when she doesn't tell her sister how she is being impacted by her sister's toxic behavior? Instead of unhealthy conversations, imagine her sister smokes and the young woman is allergic to smoke and that is what makes her sick every weekend. Should the young woman continue to put herself in harm's way without saying a word? If the conditioning she received was related to tolerating whatever family members do so that everyone can be together *no matter what*, what is this costing the young woman? How is it impacting her health and her longevity? Is being the good sister worth losing her health and maybe even her life?

Whether or not you can relate to this example, think about it for a moment. How often do we tolerate behavior from people we are *supposed* to love or get along with? And how often are we the ones made to feel guilty for our intolerance when we decide to say something or make some kind of change? These kinds of situations lead to a lot of suffering for many people. Many people end up sick as a result.

I call this kind of behavior "self-rape." It's easy for us to see the wrong in a person making inappropriate sexual advances on a non-consenting individual, yet it's hard for us to see how we allow ourselves to be harmed by others in the way they speak to us or treat us, especially family members or people in a position of authority over us. When someone screams and yells at us, these are animalistic instincts of survival that are just as harmful and damaging as someone making uninvited sexual advances.

The Buddha called these types of conditioned behaviors mental formations. We perceive and acknowledge them as something very good that we are doing, but in reality they are not good—for us or for the other person. They are instincts of survival that have been passed down, which makes the idea of them complicated. We have these instincts that have been instilled in us and we see them as positive because they fit in with the conditioned environment where they are rooted. When we act from them, we fit in that environment. This can be a beautiful thing if we do so consciously, if we understand what we are doing and why we are doing it. Most importantly, if we feel joy and peace in the moment. If, though, we are acting automatically, without any thought of why, it is a totally different experience. We are then acting from our animalistic instincts. And this is when we can harm ourselves and others.

Here's another example. Let's say your daughter has been hurt by a boy. You see her crying about what he said to her. Immediately you feel the need to protect her. If you act from animalistic instinct, you might immediately want to call the boy names to get back at him. You might even want to hurt him for the hurt he's caused your daughter. These would be automatic responses and they most likely are based on the conditioning you received in your life that says we must protect our loved ones *no matter what—no matter the cost to ourselves and those who did harm*. The intention behind your actions is beautiful—it is your desire to keep her safe. But how effective would such actions be, especially if you act from a place of rage?

Now, if you are able to act from a place of love and compassion for your daughter, and even for yourself when you want to go and hurt this boy, you'll give yourself the space to gather more information. Maybe you'll want to find out what is going on between them so you can help both kids. They may be feeling overwhelmed or fearful and need help understanding what is going on between them. This would be a totally different response, and it is going to create a completely different reality. There is also going to be an absolutely different manifestation of the truth—a much more powerful one. Imagine that instead of going and telling the boy in a fit of rage, "You are going to die!" you are able to acknowledge your rage as natural and instinctive, but at the same time understand that you cannot act from that place of rage because it won't be good for you, for anyone else, or for the situation and its outcome. Your daughter and the boy will have the opportunity to be heard and you may be able to offer them the support they're each needing.

In being able to come to an understanding of the situation rather than react from instinct, your body chemistry will also change. It is actually going to take you from an acidic state created from the stress of your initial reaction to an alkaline one. This is extremely positive for your future longevity. In an alkaline state, the chances of becoming sick are greatly reduced. Additionally, you'll find yourself in a place of joy and peace in the end.

Instincts have their place—they serve us well when our lives are in imminent danger. In times of danger, there is often no time for contemplation of the situation. Our instincts help us decide whether to run or stay, or whether to take some kind of action. But in our day-to-day lives, those conditioned automatic responses usually do more harm than good. Our lives do not need to be as fear-based as we might think. But how do we move away from living in and acting out of fear?

7

MOVING FROM FEAR TO LOVE

MUCH OF OUR CONDITIONING is based in fear. From almost the beginning of our lives, society teaches us to be afraid. Some of that teaching is helpful. Teaching a child to be afraid of a hot stove or an electrical outlet is helpful as they are beginning to learn about their environment. Understanding that cars travel on the street where the child lives is critical information for a child who is learning to cross the street. These pieces of information, along with guidance and support from adults, help a child understand that danger does exist and must be considered and acknowledged in order to survive. There is such a thing as healthy fear. It keeps us safe. It helps us learn to navigate our world. It is instinctual, and our responses to it are instinctive. A certain amount of it is learned through our conditioning.

Yet, our perspective of what we need to fear is distorted. In order to produce a society of followers and conformists, fear is perpetuated in most aspects of our lives, whether in churches, governments, our educational systems, and even our financial institutions. Having a society of fearful people provides more guarantees that individuals and groups will comply and follow. It causes us to be more separate from one another and when we do come together, even in marriage, we enter contracts to reduce our fear. It is an animalistic instinct to keep things, and people, under control. We have been conditioned to fear and to instinctually grab on to things, such as contracts, to give us a sense of safety and security.

Fear is necessary, as long as we have a clear understanding of the reason for our fear. It is also essential that we understand why and how we respond to fear. People can have their feelings of fear and they can suffer and experience pain. People don't have to act from it, however.

Not even Jesus was without any fear when he was put on the cross. However, he did not act from it. As Jesus hung on the cross in pain, he forgave people. His actions of forgiveness have a huge significance when we consider how we normally behave as human beings, because he went against his animalistic instinct. Acting from instinct would have looked a lot different. Jesus might have been screaming and maybe even swearing at those who put him there. Instead, he let everyone know he was here to forgive and to offer love. He demonstrated in the biggest way that although he was about to die he did not act from the fear he was feeling. He did not lash out at anyone or withdraw. He was present to what was happening to him and to those around him. In my opinion, he showed us how to acknowledge fear and suffering and move beyond it to show love and compassion for those involved, including himself. He was able to move beyond his instincts to show us the highest form of love—loving even as his life was slipping away.

Let's take a look at another aspect of fear. We often confuse instinct with intuition. Instinct is always based on the past and the future. Intuition is always based on what is happening now—in the present. Let me give you an example. Let's say that your teenage daughter went to a party. She didn't come home at the time she was supposed to. Your head is going to fill in all the empty spaces, all the places in your mind of "I don't know what has happened." In those spaces, your mind will go to what happened to her in the past, and even what happened to you. Maybe at the same age she is now, you had a bad experience and were physically harmed. That instinct of protection based on the past is going to cause you to worry. Again, the instinct is not a bad thing. It is going to help you remember what happened previously and even feel what you felt then. It might lead you to decide to go out and look for her. It will definitely lead to your heart rate speeding up and your breathing changing. Something connected to the past instinctively wants you to make sure that she will be safe in the future. And that leads you to want to get control of what is happening right now to stop events from leading to her harm.

Intuition, on the other hand, is a deep knowing that has nothing to do with past events or looking to the future. Here's an example. Your child is at school and suddenly you have this feeling that something is wrong. You just *know* that something is going on. Nobody has given you any information and there is nothing happening to cause you to have this sense. Without any explanation or any information or any need to fill in blanks in your mind, you simply know. That is intuition. A deep sense of knowing something without any input from anywhere, including the past or future. It is a perfect present moment. Maybe when you pick her up from school later in the day you find out she had a bloody nose but because it was resolved there was no need to call you.

In the example above related to your teenager, the moment you bring your intuition into the situation is the moment you are able to say, "I am acknowledging that I am experiencing this feeling because it is very uncomfortable. Most likely, I am remembering something that happened in the past." That gives you the opportunity to decipher whether the fear coming up is real in the moment or based on past experiences. You can then use your energy in a positive way to deal with the situation rather than begin to freak out, screaming and crying and panicking.

These instinctive, emotionally-charged responses are usually the kinds of reactions people have. You begin to cry, you begin to sweat, your adrenaline pumps, and your heart beats like crazy as the feeling of desperation builds within you. Based on past experiences, you work yourself into a panic, not knowing what you can or should do. None of this is going to help your daughter, but somehow you've been conditioned to believe that this worrying and fretting is useful. A big lie!

Think about it. How is screaming, crying, and freaking out going to help whatever may be going on with your daughter? Maybe she's actually having the most beautiful moment in her life with a friend. She may be with her friend having an intimate, deep conversation while you are at home going crazy and destroying your health. If you act on your worry and call or search for her, not only are you doing damage to yourself, but you will damage and destroy her moment and maybe your relationship with her. All because you remembered something that happened to you when you were a teenager. A very egotistical response, by the way, because it is based on you and your needs rather than her true well-being.

I am not suggesting that parents should never check up on their children and ensure that they are safe. As parents, we want to do the best we can to ensure our children's safety. I am, however, suggesting that when we do this and discover that all was well, we need to update our hard drives with this new, more current, more accurate information based on our children's behavior rather than our past personal experiences. Maybe the next time a situation arises, before you go into instinctual reaction, you can ask yourself, "How many times have I reacted instinctively? How many times did the reality of the situation match my mind's imaginings? How many times was my fear disproportionate to what was really happening? Has this behavior served and made my family more healthy and happy?"

Without criticism for how you've handled situations in the past you can use the clarity you've gained in reality to check in with yourself before going into a response. Once more, this is an opportunity to acknowledge the signal and bring in your deepest intuition to determine what, if any, action is warranted. It is an opportunity to clarify the difference between your instinct and your intuition. It is the opportunity for your actions to be based in love rather than fear. Each time you are able to create space before acting instinctively by asking yourself a question such as, "How will this behavior serve my family and make everyone more happy and healthy?" you have the opportunity to respond from your heart, using your intuition. Such a response changes your and your child's internal chemistry. And the communication between your child and you is going to be improved as well. Each time you are able to respond from a place of love rather than out of fear you create that healthier alkaline environment, internally and externally.

The goal is not to deny our fear. As human beings, we have and experience fear. We also possess our animalistic instincts. Whenever we deny our instincts and our nature we risk acting even more inappropriately. We also risk becoming ill because we are trying to contain something that cannot be suppressed. We cannot stop our true nature any more than we can stop water from overflowing the banks of a river that is filled to capacity. It is never about fighting our true nature. Because when we fight against our instincts and our innate nature, we are fighting ourselves. And that is a battle we cannot win.

Let me offer one last example. As a society, we talk about fighting diseases. We do this because we have an instinctual fear of the disease and the possibility of dying. Rather than acknowledge that we are afraid, we say we're going to fight. We're even encouraged to do so. Sometimes people say to the person who is sick that they need to put up "the fight of their life." And everyone who loves that person gets behind them and offers encouragement for them to fight as hard as they can. Again, what are they fighting in actuality? Themselves, of course. What if, instead of fighting the disease, we were able to embrace it? What if, with love, compassion, and understanding, we were able to say that although we are afraid, we are going to embrace the disease and the treatment and see that this experience is being offered to us for our growth as a person? How might that approach change the chemistry, the landscape of our bodies? How might that focus even change the outcome?

The shift we are striving for is to be able to acknowledge that we have fear, to be able to say in certain circumstances, "I am afraid," but then to pause and ask, "What am I going to do? What actions will come from the **HIGHER** me and be for my highest good and for the highest good of others?" This shift allows us to respond with love, compassion, and understanding—for ourselves and everyone involved—rather than react like an animal. Those three ingredients—love, compassion, and understanding—create the magic and represent love in action. Rather than filling in the blanks of that which we do not know, we have the opportunity to be at peace with that which is.

8

BRIDGES OF ASSUMPTIONS

IN THE LAST CHAPTER, we looked at how our minds can fill in information when we have gaps between what we know and what we don't know. Our minds are not able to function when there are gaps. Our minds are linear machines, so anytime we have a gap in what the mind knows it wants to fill it in with something. The way our heads deal with the gaps is to fill in those empty spaces with all kinds of assumptions based on our experiences.

In the previous chapter we talked about the teenager who didn't come home at the time she was supposed to. The parent filled in the spaces of his/her mind with information based on his/her own previous bad experience. This led to assumptions about what was happening at the moment to the daughter. The parent also made assumptions about what had been happening while the daughter was out and what was going to happen next. None of those assumptions were based in reality—they were simply conjectures based on the parent's past. And they met the parent's need to fill in what was not known.

From the very beginning of trying to answer what we don't know, it's important for us to understand that our assumptions are not real. They are never true. They are not based on what is happening in the present moment—and they are always related to the past or the future.

Occasionally our assumptions can match up with reality. For instance, I might assume that what is in your cup is tea and then it turns out you are in fact drinking tea. Until I confirm that you are drinking tea, however, it is not real. In actuality, my assumption is never real. It is just pure luck that my mind filled in the blank with what you were actually drinking. Maybe I knew that the restaurant where you're having something to drink is famous for their teas, so I assume that you must be drinking tea for that reason. Or maybe I've seen you drink tea before at that time of day. Occasionally, our assumptions end up being the same as reality, but that does not make our assumptions real—they never are. Unfortunately, our egos love when our minds get it right. The mind feels even stronger in its ability to fill in the blanks.

Assumptions are like a GPS. The GPS is not the road. It is an image. And it only works when we actually get into the car and begin a trip. We cannot go to Miami, for instance, staying in our room with our GPS. We have to go out and take the trip. The GPS is incomplete information. It is an image of the road. And we must be in our vehicle in order for it to provide information. Even if it is the most accurate GPS in the world, it is still not the road. It never will be. And to function, it requires us to be moving. Yet, because the GPS tells us to turn right, turn left, or go straight, and it tells us exactly where we are and where we are going, we think it is real—that it *is* a representation of the road. This is what we do when we fill in the empty spaces with information from the past. For instance, when we worry about our daughter staying out past her curfew, we fill in the gap with the thoughts that something bad is happening to her. How real is the GPS? How real is the information from the past that we tell ourselves?

An assumption is a mental image. We create these assumptions to fill in the spaces of things we do not know. There is usually an element of fear in our assumptions, because we fill in the information with past experiences that we are afraid might reoccur, experiences that we actually want to avoid. That is why they are usually fearful in nature.

So how does this system of assumptions work? When the mind gets information, it needs that information to be received as a linear signal, moving in a continuous line with no end point. When this linear signal has a little space in it, a gap, the mind cannot function. The gap serves as a glitch in the mind's functionality. In order for it to operate, the mind has to create a little bridge. In this linear signal, the bridge that is created consists of an imaginary thing—an assumption. The assumption serves the mind's needs by filling in the empty space of what we do not know with something, some kind of information, in order that the "what we do knows" can be linked together. We need the "I do not knows" filled in to satisfy the mind.

Think about it for a moment. You never have an assumption about something that you know for sure. It is impossible because you do not need it. Not even if you try, will you create an assumption about something that you know for certain. There is no gap to fill in when you already know something. Because our minds are linear, going from one thing to the next in a very straight and direct way, we only use assumptions when the mind encounters a spot where there is blank space. The mind needs to fill in those gaps so that the mind can continue along its linear path, and assumptions serve to create those bridges to keep the mind moving. The bridges of assumptions are fake because the assumptions are unreal, but the system works because the bridges keep the mind going. That's why even though the assumptions are based in fear, we feel better. It's as if our minds do a big sigh of relief as soon as a bridge is created. No matter how scary the assumption may feel there is a sense of release in having some kind of information. When the mind is able to say, "Oh, now I understand," there's a sense of everything being okay, even though what was created is fake and based in fear. The mind loves to have everything figured out—everything under control. So anytime the mind can say, "Ah, now I know," the mind is satisfied, because it feels that it has regained that sense of control.

We create assumptions as a way to survive. So, once more, it takes love and compassion to understand that this mechanism is what our minds need in order to function. When we are able to see that we've created an assumption, then it's important to see it for what it is. We can allow the present moment to tell us what is true and what is an assumption.

We are not going to stop creating assumptions and again, as a mechanism of survival, they can be useful. They are a tool. They provide us with information meant to help us survive. When we can see our assumptions as just that, and not as reality, they can help us discern what is happening in the present when we don't automatically know. They give us the opportunity to look at information from the past along with what is happening in the present moment. If we are able to understand the role our assumptions serve, we do not have to instinctually respond to them. We can take them in as one more piece of information to consider.

It's important for us to observe that our assumptions come from the mind and therefore they are limited. They are not real; they are not the truth. Like our car that cannot fly us to Hawaii, our assumptions come with very specific limitations. And just as it would not be helpful for us to believe that our car will fly us to Hawaii next week, it causes us a lot of suffering when we believe our assumptions are truth—when we believe that they are an actual picture of our current reality.

Believing something as fact when it is not creates a distortion and a certain friction. This is why it is so important to understand that assumptions have their place—they help our mind function—but they are *only* a tool, and one of many tools we have. When we believe our assumptions are *everything* and when we allow them to multiply, we enter the danger zone. They are like a fire. The more we allow our assumptions to multiply it's as if we are adding oxygen to the fire. With that increase comes more suffering for us. We actually create the situations of suffering that we are trying so hard to avoid.

We don't need to extinguish the fire, to silence our assumptions, but we do need to tend the fire and keep it contained. That balance comes with our ability to enter the present moment in the midst of our assumptions. In these moments of deep analysis in the present, we can ask ourselves, "Is this assumption true?" With deep curiosity, we can continue to contemplate what is happening: "Am I assuming something? Is that assumption coming from the past? Is that assumption relevant to the present? What is actually happening in the present?" This is your heart, your intuition, coming into the conversation. Your heart, which is hungry for truth and vibrates in truth, can help analyze what is going on. Your mind vibrates in what it does and doesn't like, which is why it goes to the past to fill in those blanks. Your heart, however, when it is allowed expression, is truth itself manifesting through you.

With your heart's help, you can begin to get comfortable with the spaces. You can begin to explore why you needed to create that assumption in the first place. Many times they are based on our expectations. In actuality, expectations are assumptions. The bigger the expectations, the more suffering they create. When the teenage daughter did not come home on time, the parent had an expectation that she would. When the expectation wasn't met, the parent began to suffer. The mind created all kinds of assumptions in addition to the original expectation to fill in why the daughter was late, which led to more suffering.

Here's another example from childhood. Remember being taken to an ice cream parlor and ordering your favorite ice cream. Your childhood self was so excited that as the server prepared your ice cream cone, your mouth began to water. You could already taste the ice cream. You giggled and squealed with delight in anticipation of your special treat. As you reached for the cone filled with two scoops of ice cream, it tipped and the ice cream fell to the floor. You began to cry as you stared at your ice cream splattered on the ground. What is the reason you cried? Did you cry because the ice cream landed on the floor? No, you cried because your expectation was destroyed by reality. You cried because you made an assumption—filling in the space of waiting—of what your ice cream would taste like when it reached your mouth. Two different things happened—your expectation/assumption and reality. This is the reason we suffer. Our heart does not suffer with the truth. Our suffering happens when the illusion created by our minds is destroyed. Our assumptions and our expectations are all illusions.

Expectations of pleasurable experiences create a certain chemistry in our body. With that anticipation come feelings of excitement and thrill, maybe even creating butterflies in our stomach. When those expectations are not fulfilled, our chemistry changes radically and we feel that as well. We can become depressed or sad or feel betrayed because our expectations were not fulfilled. We are used to this cycle of feeling high and euphoric and then plummeting to despair. When our assumptions turn out to match reality, when our expectations are met, we are accustomed to the feeling of satisfaction that comes with that result. Neither outcome, though, gives us that sense of euphoria we felt during the anticipation of our expectations.

As a society, we are addicted to this cycle, especially to the euphoria we feel, and we see this cycle as the way our minds work. We have the belief that these ways of using the mind are the right ways. We feel that this cycle is a success because we are *continuing to SURVIVE*. Each time our assumptions and expectations match reality, we believe we are doing great.

The truth is that in minimizing your assumptions and expectations, you will suffer less. The goal for each of us is to assume less and to have fewer expectations. The goal is to live in reality rather than illusion. Your mind will always bring you assumptions and offer expectations. Remember, that is its job. But whenever you can remember that assumptions and expectations create problems and suffering for you, you can respect those assumptions and expectations for what they are—just tools, pieces of information. Then, you can bring in your heart, your intuition, to discern the truth, which is what we are always seeking. There is a flexibility that comes into play as we allow our heart into the process and that makes life much sweeter. When we can live life with that flexibility, when we can become more comfortable with the "I don't know" of life, when we can release our need to have things happen in a very specific way, we will have a totally different experience of life.

Our flexibility releases us from the need to fill in the spaces with all the crazy images our assumptions can lead us to—we don't have to expend incredible amounts of energy as our mind fills in the spaces with all kinds of wild scenarios. Think about it for a moment. You've allowed your mind to go wild and your adrenaline, along with norepinephrine[*] and cortisol[**], are pumping like crazy as you try to figure out where your daughter is, and then your daughter walks in and you experience this immediate sense of relief. However, you also have this incredible amount of hormone rushing through

---

[*] Norepinephrine *n*: Also called noradrenaline. Physiology. a neurotransmitter, released by adrenergic nerve terminals in the autonomic and possibly the central nervous system, that has such effects as constricting blood vessels, raising blood pressure, and dilating bronchi.

[**] Cortisol *n*: a steroid hormone, in the glucocorticoid class of hormones, produced in humans by the zona fasciculata of the adrenal cortex within the adrenal gland. It is released in response to stress and low blood glucose. It functions to increase blood sugar through gluconeogenesis, to suppress the immune system, and to aid in the metabolism of fat, protein, and carbohydrate. It also decreases bone formation.

your body. And these hormones don't go away automatically with your sense of relief. They will stay there for quite some time—maybe even for a whole day. You may continue to feel the effects for a number of hours—things like a dry mouth or the need to take deep breaths. All because you let your mind run like wildfire with assumptions!

Whenever we are able to bring in the space of more flexibility, we avoid the suffering we experience when things don't go the way we thought they would or should. Flexibility is important because it helps us avoid both the friction and the suffering. It helps us keep our bodies from being overrun by these stress hormones as we imagine the worst. It offers the opportunity for a deeper understanding that the assumption is not real. It provides the space of understanding that there is nothing for us to control and nothing for us to do immediately in that moment.

Allowing for the space of flexibility, for the pause necessary so that your heart and intuition can have a say, helps you keep the assumptions and survival instincts in check. Since your mind is not going to stop trying to fill in the empty spaces, developing practices to assist the mind can be most helpful. In the case of waiting up for your daughter, you may not be capable of doing something like meditation or yoga as you wait, although this is absolutely possible, but doing something to fill in the space with laughter, enjoyment, or fun can help the mind cope. Whether it's eating an ice cream, putting on music and dancing in your living room, watching a comedy on television, or reading a book for entertainment, any activity that creates expansiveness in you will create a completely different chemistry in your body—a very conscious way of bridging the empty spaces of your mind.

This is not what we've been taught to do. Because of our conditioning, most of us think that wringing our hands, crying, wailing, and worrying are how to cope with these kinds of situations and support our children. Our parents and grandparents survived doing these things, so why can't we? And as a society, we're addicted to those surges of stress hormones. We may think we don't want to experience them, but the bridges of assumptions we are conditioned to create actually lead to such a chemical release. So, in order to make changes in how we create bridges in our minds, we have to go through a type of withdrawal, which is uncomfortable. Not only is it uncomfortable for the individual who begins to do things differently, but it is uncomfortable for everyone connected to that individual and the original conditioning. When the messaging you've received says that to show love for your child you must succumb to fear and exhibit worry, suddenly dancing around the living room as you wait up is going to seem strange. Not only might you question your own behavior, others looking at you may think you've lost your mind.

With all we are learning about how our minds and brains work, however, we now understand that we have the opportunity to respond differently than our conditioning alone would have us do. Every time we are able to respond with flexibility and from our hearts, every time we are able to acknowledge our mind's usual patterns but then allow space for a different response, we create new neuro pathways for how to process information. We are actually rewiring ourselves. The beautiful thing about being able to make these changes is that in the process, we are creating a better human being—a more enlightened being—a more spiritual version of ourselves.

PART THREE

THE INGREDIENTS
OF A SPIRITUAL LIFE

9

JOY AND HAPPINESS

THERE ARE MANY BOOKS about happiness and just as many books about joyfulness. They sound as if they are the same, but in reality when you study them, they are not. We are discovering more and more that there is a difference between being happy and being joyful. Even though we used to treat them as the same, we are continuing to learn that there are significant differences.

As mentioned in earlier chapters, our minds need to gather pleasure in order to survive. People confuse happiness with pleasure. For example, what makes people happy? *I'm happy when you give me what I want. I'll be happy when I graduate. I'm happy if I get the new iPhone. I'm happy if I'm with the most beautiful woman at the party. I'm happy if I have more. I'm happy if you say you love me.* All of these whens and ifs, if we analyze them, are connected to pleasure.

What is happiness then? The "happiness" that most people are searching for is not in reality really happiness. In reality, what a person is usually looking for is a certain kind of pleasure or satisfaction to feed the ego. Why is this so important? Because *in reality* this is what we were designed to do. The body was designed to gather pleasure (almost like a trophy that you receive from ∞). That pleasure is like a little reward when you are doing something that collaborates with life—with survival—something that gives you life or helps you be more alive.

The two most basic examples of pleasure are food and sex. When it comes to food, we like it so much because we feel intense pleasure when we eat good food. We experience that sense of pleasure because we are contributing to the body getting the nutrients it needs to survive—to be strong and to be alive. Sex is the other example. Probably the most pleasurable thing that a human can do in life is to have sex. We enjoy it as much as we do because it promotes life. It's one of the greatest pleasures because it's the most significant way for humans to contribute to the continuation of life. It opens us to the possibility to bring another human being into the world.

If we think about it, it's a very healthy practice to focus on gathering pleasure instead of pain. Usually this feeling of pleasure is what people are seeking, and the fulfillment of this search is what many people believe to be happiness. Over time, though, these mechanisms become distorted. Our desire to seek pleasure becomes confused with our craving to be happy. For example, in an attempt for the body system to get vitamins, proteins, and nutrients this distortion can make a person seek the pleasure of eating a whole pizza piled high with a lot of cheese. Because it is a fake sense of happiness, we not only need a lot but in a matter of time we begin to need more. And then we don't even feel satisfied or content unless we have more. When that pattern happens, it is not real happiness. It is momentary pleasure that is unsustainable. My body tells me to eat the pizza because I *do* need nutrients and nourishment, but what gets distorted is how much and how often I eat it. So, what becomes a distortion is a person's intention. It can make you believe that the body needs large amounts of pizza, for instance, in order to survive, when in reality the body gets addicted to certain chemicals in the food. In the case of the pizza, the body becomes addicted to the sugar and fats, and that is why we always need more of it.

The same mechanism can be repeated with emotions. For example, "I'll be happy when I finish this project. I'm not going to be happy now. I'm going to be happy when the project is completed and turns out the way I want." This perspective is an instinctual mechanism that has helped the person survive. It has helped them be successful. Because when we work like that, with a goal and a deadline, we make our boss happy. And when we make our boss happy, we get our little paycheck each week. The issue is that we don't feel good about what we're doing *until* certain things happen.

In both instances, people gather pleasure and feel good about the pleasure *for a while.* Because they feel good for a period of time, they continue to go back for more, but then after more time passes they're unhappy again. Even if they have the best pizza in Italy or the best job in the world, they eventually become unhappy. And that's because what they're doing is gathering pleasure, and that pleasure is conditional and temporary.

There is a cycle that gets repeated over and over in order to feel this sense of pleasure. When our feeling of "happiness" goes away, we are forced to go after it again. We know it's fun, so we put a lot of energy into getting that feeling back. Then we get it again and then it feels really good … again. The reason it feels so good is because our body is under the effects of certain endorphins and chemicals. When we feel those chemicals they feel awesome—they feel extremely pleasurable and we cannot deny that feeling.

Hormones and pheromones make us feel as if we're in heaven when we experience something pleasurable. It feels real—and in that moment the pleasure *is* real. The reason why it's so real is because in that moment we don't want anything else. We feel satisfied and satiated.

For instance, when you're having the experience of drinking something really pleasurable—such as a rich-flavored, high quality tea—most likely you're not thinking or wanting anything else. When you have an orgasm, it is not possible to be thinking that you need to pay a bill or that you want to buy a diamond. Even if the "thing" is something beautiful, there is no way to get into the chemistry of still wanting something else in that moment, because your mind is not able to "try" for anything else. When you have an orgasm you are completely engaged in that moment of pleasure.

Happiness never comes from pleasure, but we're conditioned to believe that it does. From our earliest moments, our minds were conditioned to believe that we are happy when we get the feeling of a certain chemistry and we get this chemistry when we get what we want. We are conditioned to believe in this way and then we suffer because we're constantly searching for that happiness and the feeling of the chemistry. Unfortunately, we search for this happiness in the wrong places, and we cultivate happiness in the wrong way. From a very young age, we are trained to believe that we will be happy when we get something. *You'll be happy when you get the lollipop you want. You'll be happy when you get the ice cream. You'll be happy when you get the partner you want. You'll be happy when you become the person that you've always wanted to be* (because you're never that person in the moment).

It's always something that's going to happen in the future—like a donkey going after a carrot—and that's never complete happiness. It's just a glimpse of happiness that happens for a brief moment. So that happiness is very limited and very incomplete. That's why it feels as if it is always a moving target. We get it and we lose it. We get it and we lose it. We put a lot of energy into getting it again, and then—Wow!—we lose it again. This is because, as the Buddha realized, everything is always changing. It's changing now and it's going to change in the future. Even if you win the lottery and think you're finally going to be happy—it's going to change. Even if you have a terminal illness—it's going to change. Of course, the things that we don't want to change—like winning the lottery and being rich—don't feel good when they do change. But in the case of a terminal illness, we can welcome that change and see it as positive. No matter how we perceive something, though, things change. Nothing can last. When something is conditional—whether we see it as positive or negative—it is not real. When something is conditional, it is obviously limited—not bad, but limited. Therefore, what we seek as pleasure is limited. It cannot last.

It feels to me that there is a different kind of happiness, though, and I call that happiness *joy*. It's the happiness that doesn't depend on external stimuli. It's the happiness that doesn't depend on whether I get what I want or not.

Here is an example of something that made me understand this concept in a deeper way. Let's say that what you want is a million dollars. You win the lottery and you get ten million dollars. From your perspective, that amount of money will make you totally free of problems—it represents even more than you originally desired. If you have the ten million dollars and you're not in touch with the *joy* that I'm talking about, though, you're going to become miserable. It's only a matter of time before the money will create a living hell.

When you study the lives of people who have a lot of money, they often have a lot of misery and pain. Again, it isn't that the money is bad or that having a lot of money is not a good thing. But if I gather the money and I don't gather this *joy*, the money will be useless. "Money" can represent all kinds of things—your social status, the house you want, the car you want, the partner you want. Everything is touched by that concept of "money."

I discovered this other happiness, this *joy* that I'm talking about, by understanding that what makes me happy is not wanting or gathering anything. It is never about seeking something. That kind of pleasure that we seek is incomplete. This *limited happiness* is relative and dualistic. When something is relative or dualistic, it is obviously not something that is realistic. Yet, that's what almost everyone is searching for ... even in most people's spiritual search. This *limited happiness* is what most people are searching for when they get married, when they have children, when they buy a house, when they purchase a painting, or even when they get into spiritual practices.

Since pleasure (*limited happiness*) is something that all of us contend with, in my teachings I like to create a way to distinguish between it and *joy*. So, when faced with a pleasurable experience, I invite people to ask, "Is this joy or is this happiness/pleasure?" Otherwise, if we don't have a way to differentiate between the two, it is extremely confusing and can be extremely painful.

The joy that I'm talking about can even be felt in very difficult moments in our lives. Even in the most difficult times, you can still be joyful. You won't experience pleasure in a difficult moment, but you can experience joy. It's like the moment when you need to take your child to the hospital and the doctor has to do something that will be very painful for your child. It's difficult to go through with what needs to be done because there is no pleasure involved. But when you do it because it's necessary you feel this completeness—this joy—because you know you are doing what you have to do for your child. And you know you are being responsible.

After you execute what is the right thing to do you don't feel fear because you know you've done the best you can in the moment. You feel peace because you have no doubt, you have no questioning. You are able to say, "I'm doing the best I can at this moment," or, "I'm doing everything possible in this moment." There is no judgment because you're doing everything possible. You feel complete. You don't feel euphoric—you feel peaceful. You don't feel an adrenaline rush or a rush of the other stress hormones—you feel content. You don't feel excited or thrilled—you feel calm. This calm is very confusing for the ego, by the way, because our egos are so agitated and over-stimulated that they feel like this sense of stillness is as if we're dying. The ego wants excitement and the rush of stress hormones, and feels as if calm and peace is suicide. Yet, this calm, this peace, is pure joy.

Another example is being at a funeral, where you are not going to feel pleasure. You are never happy when you attend a funeral. But even at a funeral, you can experience joy. You can have a sense of knowing that it is right for you to be there for so many different reasons. And the result of that joy—the chemistry that is created—is a sense of peace. You feel contentment. You feel completeness.

It's been interesting to me to see people who have maybe three dollars in the bank and yet they can touch this joyfulness. So this joy is better than money. If you have the money and you don't have this other condition—this joyfulness— you will be miserable. So it is more valuable to have and experience joy than to win the lottery. It can be very painful to win this large amount of money and not be able to be joyful.

At least when you don't have the money you might hold on to the illusion that you're going to have it someday. That illusion can keep you moving forward. But when you get there, when you have the money but you don't have this sense of joy, the money will feel empty. And you will suffer even more than before you had the money. Instead of being at peace, you will be worried about losing your money. Or you will worry about how to invest it in the right way. Or you will worry about someone stealing it from you. Or you might have the experience that now everyone only loves you and wants to hang out with you because you have ten million dollars. That has to be a really difficult, extremely painful, and very lonely way to live.

So this is the difference. Joy gives you a sense of completeness, peace, and contentment, while happiness/pleasure leaves you empty, incomplete, and always wanting more.

When you begin to practice and get more in touch with that peace than with the pleasure, there is something that can happen in the body hormonally. You can actually feel what a real spiritual experience feels like—pure ecstasy. This is not the same "ecstasy" that you get when you do drugs, for example, or the "ecstasy" that is felt in something extremely pleasurable. When you begin to experience this "ecstasy," it doesn't feel like a thrill, it doesn't feel like "Wow! This is good." With time, though—when you experience that sense of peace and joy more and more—the body begins to develop a very interesting chemistry. It is a chemistry that can actually be seen externally. When the person is in total ecstasy, it becomes visible to others and impacts everything and everyone that the person is in contact with. Even if everything is totally crazy outside and around the person, the individual can be literally in total peace, which is total ecstasy.

You cannot expect to feel this ecstasy overnight or in the first weeks or months of practicing. If you expect it to happen immediately, you're searching for the wrong thing— this ecstasy that I'm speaking about is not an experience of pleasure. Often people seek spiritual paths because they are looking for pleasure; they want to learn how to have pleasure even if horrible things are going on in their lives. Spirituality doesn't work that way.

What usually happens when someone begins to touch this state of joyfulness is that initially a person begins to sleep better—they are able to go to sleep and really rest. Their sleeping patterns change, because of the chemistry that is changing. They feel less resistance about life. So, if they're a little depressed, for example, it begins to go away. It's like an undertone of everything being okay. If we analyze this, we see that it is the person becoming okay with what is real. They begin to have a better relationship with what is instead of wanting reality to be the way they want it to be. There's a sense of "okayness" with the way things are.

The serotonin levels also change in the process, so many people who suffer from any type of physical pain, experience that their pain diminishes or even goes away completely. Much of this pain happens because of this relationship with pushing and pushing and struggling. When they stop pushing and struggling, the pain dissipates.

People also begin to have a better relationship with their body, a more loving and compassionate relationship with what is happening in their body, especially something difficult, instead of continuing to do the same thing and expecting that they will automatically have a better result. Instead of taking a pill to cover up their pain. Instead of pushing through, no matter what. If someone has been experiencing pain, they begin to be able to listen to their body and to have love and compassion for what is happening. So maybe, for example, if the person loves to dance and doesn't want to stop dancing even though their knees hurt, they decide to change the music, or the type of dance, or the frequency of dancing rather than give up dancing completely.

There are other hormones and chemicals that begin to change the way they reproduce within the body as well. Dopamine* and many others begin to be produced in a more balanced way, because the person is having a better relationship within themselves and with life outside themselves.

Every living being wants a sense of peace and, basically, you cannot have sustainable happiness if you do not have this peace. You can have the money, the most expensive car, the most expensive house, or the finest tea. You can have everything, but if you do not have this sense of peace, that happiness/pleasure is temporary and becomes boring.

All spiritual teachers invite you to cultivate this peace. This lasting peace is the peace that Jesus was offering us. This is the peace that the Buddha was asking us to seek. This is the *sakinah* that in the Koran is the most important feeling. The whole Koran is about cultivating this peace. Hinduism invites you to get out of the dualistic mind and be peaceful. When you destroy all of that—good/bad, right/wrong, your way/ my way—you become peaceful. Letting go of duality allows you to be peaceful.

It doesn't matter what religion you practice. It doesn't matter what temple or church you attend. If you do not have this peace, you have nothing. Because we are usually seeking religion and spirituality from that place of happiness/pleasure, we don't really take the nectar that all these religions offer. All religions and spiritual paths have beautiful aspects. When you study them, you discover treasures and diamonds,

---

* Dopamine *n*: Biochemistry. a catecholamine neurotransmitter in the central nervous system, retina, and sympathetic ganglia, acting within the brain to help regulate movement and emotion: its depletion may cause Parkinson's disease.

but if what you're searching for is the next "pleasure," then the religion or spiritual path will be meaningless—because it won't be able to give you what you want. When you are seeking pleasure, you lose the whole point of what the religion or spiritual path has to offer. I'm not saying that any path is perfect, but it's this mistaken way we relate to our spiritual and religious quests, and not necessarily the religion or spiritual practice itself, that causes us the most suffering.

When there is no pleasure attached to the seeking of joy, when there is no instantaneous reward, then we don't necessarily seek it. But this joy is exactly what we really need. It is the cure for illnesses, for stress, for anxiety, for fear, and more.

Many people avoid meditation. Why? In my opinion, it's because they don't believe they get anything out of it. In reality, what we get is this sense of peace—this joy—and we learn to observe our mind and see what it does and where it goes. Yoga is another example. There are a thousand excuses for not doing yoga. Number one is, "I don't want to because I don't feel good." Then there are others: "I'm not flexible," "Everything hurts," "I'm too old," etc., etc. What do you get out of yoga? Nothing really … if you're seeking pleasure. If you go to yoga class to get a sculpted body, you're going to get it, but you're going to feel empty in the process.

What yoga provides, when you practice for the right reasons, is a dynamic meditation. The meaning of yoga is union. The invitation of yoga is to use your mind and your body together. The more they are able to work together, the more the yoga poses allow flexibility in you—mentally, emotionally, spiritually, and physically. In the process of creating that flexibility, you begin to see how much your mind comes in and tells you that you cannot do it. The mind that allows you to think that you are not enough—not flexible enough, not focused enough, not calm enough—attempts to trick you and limit you, but when you are able to acknowledge the mind and continue to breathe into the pose, something magical happens. These very uncomfortable positions, as you move into them, change the mental, emotional, and hormonal states in the body. You can become amazed at how this magical, dynamic meditation can stretch you. The expansion is physical and mental, and it opens the elasticity that is necessary in both the body and the mind, bringing you a sense of incredible peace and joy.

This joy and peace you feel when you practice is not something you lose when you die. Everything you acquire materialistically in your lifetime and everything your body looks like physically, you leave here when you die. But the peace you acquire—this frequency, this energy that is your own—you take with you, and your reincarnation is going to depend on the frequency of that energy. Imagine that! You take it into your next incarnation. You take the vibration inside of you—this infinite vibration that is the real you. You attune this vibration with practice, with new beliefs, with a communion with reality. You begin to experience this sense of peace—this joy—here and now. You don't have to die to find it. In Zen Buddhism, it's called dying before you die. It is not the body dying—it's my mind dying. It's the ego—the "I am what I think"—that dies. And when that dies you discover who you are without all your thoughts, without all that you think of as "you"—your gender, your spiritual beliefs, your responsibilities, your fears, your conditioning.

In the bible it says that searchers search and search, and what the searcher encounters is going to create discomfort. So, we are invited to search and see what is. What we find is that we have to kill our beliefs. And that's uncomfortable. There's going to be discomfort, but that's the real search. The real search is not always having things go the way we want them to go. That's why people are disappointed when truth happens. They can even get mad with ∞. They try to go away from ∞ and not have any spiritual practice anymore because they didn't get what they wanted. In reality, what creates our suffering is what we carry in our heads—our beliefs, our ways of living, our desires, our expectations, our fears, our psychological patterns and conditioning. We'll be in discomfort as we begin to let go of all of these things, but in the end we will find peace. We stop what we've been doing and then we feel peaceful. We find the real us within. And that's the real search. That's the real treasure.

This joy, this peace, is so much better than any drug. It makes you feel complete. When you have it, you don't want anything. You no longer suffer because you feel fulfilled. This creates extremely powerful and dynamic movement within yourself that allows you to manifest your real purpose. That movement allows you to manifest more creativity, productivity, and responsibility, and results in improvements in all aspects of your life. Everything becomes significant, and each moment becomes everything. There is nothing before or after. There is no want of anything. Each moment is pure joy and bliss. This is the real experience of heaven.

10

THE MIDDLE WAY

IN THE LAST CHAPTER we looked at the significance of finding peace and joy in our lives, and now we will explore that the only way to do that is to find our individual Middle Way.* It is the way that the Buddha found, and it is a beautiful way to live. The other great teachers found their Middle Way as well. Jesus, for instance, found his Middle Way through his actions—he showed us that he was human. He showed us that he could get mad like any other human being. Yet, he had to find his Middle Way that allowed him to feel joy and peace during his lifetime and even at the time of his death.

This Middle Way is a total acceptance of who we are without trying to make anything better, without trying to make a better version of ourselves, because we're already perfect. It's knowing that every person is already per-

---

* Middle Way *n*: The Buddhist practice of No Extremism.

fect. This Middle Way allows us to see our humanity and embrace it with love and compassion. Our humanity is a unique opportunity that's taken eons and eons of life to develop; it's taken years and years for us to come into this form where we are this animal that is also a Buddha and a Jesus—an animal that is all the spiritual masters.

Just look at what ∞ created in us. We are animals who like food, who like pleasure, and at the same time we are interacting and communicating with each other, we are able to contemplate everything—including life itself and what lies beyond this life we're living. That's creativity!

We are each an individual expression of that creativity. Each one of us is unique. Each one of us brings our uniqueness to any and every experience. Imagine! We are nurturing ∞ through our unique selves and through our unique experiences. ∞ is watching, not to judge us, but to enjoy. You are nurturing ∞ through your experiences. That's why you're here. That's why ∞ put all of this energy for us to be here. ∞ is enjoying us—each and every one of us. It's sublime how much ∞ enjoys us, for no reason at all other than to enjoy us.

We're light beings learning how to be humans. We need to have love and compassion for that circumstance. Every unique person has work to be done, and we each have a unique reason for being here. We need to find our own unique Middle Way to allow for our unique expression of our being-ness.

Each person's Middle Way will be different. Maybe for one person it is writing, maybe for another it's singing or playing a musical instrument, maybe for another it's spending time with horses, maybe for another it's playing baseball, and for another it's becoming a teacher or a doctor. There are an infinite number of ways for each of us to find our unique expression. What is important is that we each find our own Middle Way—and not anyone else's.

Even the Buddha said we each have to find our individual unique expression. He did not suggest that anyone do it in exactly the same way as he did. When we truly allow ourselves to find our own expression, it can turn out to be very surprising, even to us. It can be something we never imagined doing or being. As long as it is our own and we feel joyful and peaceful about it, then we've found it! It is total communion with our reality, with what is in front of us, without any comparison to anyone else or even to whom we were before. There is no judgment—no right or wrong. There is only our unique Middle Way.

The process of finding our Middle Way requires the creation of space, where we can respect the primate that we are and the angel that we are—because we are both. You can call the spiritual aspect of you by whatever name you wish—whether that's an angel, or god, or goddess, or divine, or ∞. The name is not as important as being able to acknowledge that this spiritual aspect is a part of who you are as much as you are a primate. It's essential to find a unique way, as unique as you are, to create a balance with both aspects, because you cannot be only the angel or only the primate. When you go to one extreme or the other you will begin to feel the friction within yourself. For instance, if we live in the world, we cannot sit and meditate 24/7 and expect to sustain ourselves and meet our basic needs for food and shelter. We have to find the Middle Way, which is the integration of both our spiritual being-ness and our human-ness.

There is a beautiful story from the Buddha's life that portrays this concept. As the Buddha was meditating to become enlightened, he was dying because he had not eaten in a very long time. There was a beautiful girl named Sujata who was passing by with a dessert called keer. Keer is an Indian sweet milk-rice pudding. Sujata said to the Buddha, "Stop! You're dying. You're killing yourself. Eat a little. You must eat." Buddha accepted the girl's offering and ate.

Another example is a well-known story about a sitar player who was discouraged with his meditation practice. He went to the Buddha to ask for instruction.

"What happens when you tune your instrument too tightly?" Buddha asked.

"The strings break."

"And what happens when you string it too loosely?"

"When it's too loose, no sound comes out."

"The string that produces a tuneful sound is not too tight and not too loose. That," said the Buddha, "is how to practice: not too tight and not too loose." *The Middle Way*.

It's important to be careful in our lives. If we meditate only we can kill ourselves just as the Buddha almost did. We cannot, however, completely deny that spiritual part of us, that part of us that is capable of contemplation. We must therefore find our Middle Way—what will work best for each of us to bring together our spiritual nature and our human nature. We cannot focus only on one and deny the other. When we do, we risk losing our lives.

Let's look more deeply at this concept. How many times in life do we try to do something with a very beautiful intention but in the end we create suffering for ourselves? *I am an artist but my mother has held the dream that I would be a lawyer. So to make my mother happy I become a lawyer, but then my life is miserable.* That is how we miss the Middle Way. When I'm miserable my mother isn't happy and I'm not happy either. This happens a lot to people. They force themselves to do things that they know they shouldn't do or don't want to do. How do they know? Because they're extremely uncomfortable or suffering in some way, whether that is physically, emotionally, or both. The Middle Way respects the signal from the beginning—it represents the person's own boundaries. When we don't respect this signal, we get ourselves into trouble.

The difficulty is that we are culturally pushed and we push ourselves. We don't respect our limits. This is what our culture and our families want us to do, but then we suffer. The Middle Way is finding something that doesn't harm anyone—ourselves or others. The Middle Way is your own. The Middle Way is never anyone else's Middle Way. The Middle Way is going to be unique to you. Society and institutions want us to conform but that is not the Middle Way. The Middle Way is something very delicate, and nobody can tell another person what his or her Middle Way needs to be. We each have to discover it for ourselves. We can find guidance from the great teachers. Through their lives, they have taught us to live the Middle Way, but the true teachers also show us that we must find our own way. You and I won't do exactly what they did.

The Middle Way relates to everything in our lives. It relates to our life's purpose, to the work we do in the world, to how we conduct ourselves each and every day, to the relationships we maintain, and to every decision we make—no matter how big or small. This Middle Way becomes a part of our daily lives. It becomes the way we live and relate in the world day in and day out. Our Middle Way becomes a part of who we are in every moment.

The Middle Way is not denying another person's thoughts, ideas, and feelings, but it is also not doing what they want if it denies our own feelings. Sometimes it will be uncomfortable for us or for others, but if it is our Middle Way it will feel peaceful. Because the Middle Way is not a compromise, it takes everything into consideration. The person is able to see a bigger picture.

The Middle Way, therefore, is not going to be a compromise between me and another person. It means that in each situation, I will take into consideration the information that another person offers, but it doesn't mean I will follow that information blindly or create a compromise between what they offer and what I desire. A Middle Way is not synonymous with finding middle ground. The Middle Way also doesn't mean I will only listen to my ego and be selfish—disregarding any information that is offered to me. Not taking into account anyone else's perspective actually represents flipping the coin—and that is not the Middle Way either.

A person has to find a way to do what makes that person feel peaceful. You can't do something only to make someone else happy. Nor can you act from a place of not caring what anybody else thinks or feels or says. Neither of these approaches will make you feel peaceful. If you're going to disregard other people or any living being and that causes them to suffer as a result of your actions, it's never a peaceful deal. It may feel good in the moment but it won't give you lasting peace. Our actions have to be followed by that sense of peace. When they are, then we are in our Middle Way.

Finding our Middle Way doesn't necessarily mean that other people won't suffer as a result of our decisions and actions. Not everyone will agree with our Middle Way. But as long as we are feeling peaceful rather than feeling a temporary sense of pleasure, we know we're in our Middle Way. As long as we have taken others' ideas and feelings into consideration as well as our own, we can feel that sense of peace, regardless of the outcome of our Middle Way. Let me give you an example.

Let's say you are planning to travel outside of the country with your family, which includes your young children. In order to travel to certain regions, it is recommended that you receive certain vaccinations prior to your departure. These vaccinations are not required but strongly recommended. You take that into consideration as well as the risks involved with receiving or not receiving the vaccinations. You also take into account the pain your child will experience from the injection and the potential illness your child might experience if they do not receive the vaccination. You even take into account the potential reactions they might have to the vaccination itself. In order to decide, if you are following your Middle Way, you will ask yourself, "Which one can I live with more peacefully? Which decision will give me a sense of peace?"

Whether or not you have your family take the vaccinations, there is always a chance that someone might become ill—maybe even a 50/50 chance. They may become ill as a result of the vaccination itself or as a result of not taking the vaccination. So, again, the question is which decision will make you feel more peaceful. It's worth looking at all the information, because once you make your decision, you will ultimately have that sense of peace for having made the best decision possible. Even if your child is angry or scared about having to receive an injection. Even if you have a sense of fear about the potential for illness. It's not about *preferring* that someone else, such as your child, suffer and that you don't suffer, but it is about making certain that you will not suffer as a result of your decision, *even if* the other person does. It is you being at peace with your Middle Way, without any sense of guilt. You understand someone else's pain and you have compassion for it, but you still have to follow your Middle Way.

If we go back to the example from Jesus' life, many people suffered as a result of his death—especially his mother, I imagine. I'm sure he took that into consideration. I'm sure he considered how his death would impact all those he loved, all the people closest to him. Yet, he ultimately had to do what would bring him the most peace. He was not without fear but he knew that in order to help others and live out his life's purpose, he had to allow himself to be hung on the cross. That was Jesus' Middle Way.

The Middle Way is a more challenging place to live from—especially as we first begin to do this in our life. It is tougher to begin to live the Middle Way, because we usually don't want to take the whole picture into consideration, including our personal responsibility, when making a decision. We usually deny ourselves completely or deny other people, and we deny much of the information available to us. The Middle Way takes thought, it takes creating a space between the situation and the decision—so it takes time and energy. We have to consider our thoughts and beliefs as well as other people's thoughts and beliefs, along with the circumstances of the situation. We have to be conscious of everything before choosing the Middle Way.

Rather than allowing for this space, we often go into our defense mechanisms, which allow us to do what we want without taking the whole picture into account. Sometimes, in the process, we bend completely to what other people want us to do, with total disregard for ourselves. At times, flipping the coin in this way is what we have to do to begin to make progress. Sometimes the scale is balanced one way and then we have to go completely the other way to create some change. These are indications of a healthy ego. That energy, that movement, is progress—and helps us eventually get to balance. Sometimes the pendulum has to swing the complete opposite way, or back and forth, before it can move to the Middle Way.

So, when we are striving to find our Middle Way, we have to have love and compassion for ourselves and remember that our conditioning and our automatic defense mechanisms are there. Can we expect that our mind will forget everything it's known? Of course not. Although we want to get to the place where we don't suffer anymore, that's not really possible because we will always have our conditioning and automatic defense mechanisms as part of us. The more we evolve as humans, though, the more we will learn how to have a better understanding of ourselves. We can begin to have a different relationship with those automatic elements. We can continue to know them better and acknowledge that they are there, without automatically engaging with them. We observe; we give ourselves space—a buffer—before we react.

When we only listen to our heads we get into trouble. If we deny everyone else, we get into trouble too. So it's with love and compassion that we must take everything and everyone into account before taking an action, including ourselves and our conditioning. Our Middle Way is a work in progress.

Our Middle Way is also always changing. It's essential that we allow for that change. The litmus test will continue to be whether or not we are feeling peaceful in any given moment. The Middle Way will never have anything to do with pleasure or pain—it will always give us a feeling of peace. In order to allow for an evolving Middle Way, flexibility is absolutely necessary. There is not one instrument that measures balance that doesn't include flexibility. Within the process of finding our Middle Way, and in maintaining our Middle Way, we therefore must be flexible. That flexibility creates the balance.

Life is continually changing. That is the nature of life. In order for us not to suffer, we must be able to be flexible and change along with life. If we do that with love, compassion, and respect for ourselves, for others, and for life itself, we will continue to find our Middle Way.

There are other qualities required to maintain our Middle Way. Strength is one of those qualities. Yet, strength alone is not sufficient. Consider these questions:

**What is the value of strength
if there's no flexibility?
What happens if you have strength
and flexibility at the same time?**

Think about what it takes for a building to withstand an earthquake. Buildings that are built to allow for both strength and flexibility are able to endure earthquakes. Buildings that are built only for strength, such as a building made of cement, will collapse and crumble, but those buildings that are created as a result of being mindful about their need to sustain movement, endure. Most of today's buildings are created with that in mind. Both strength and flexibility are designed into the structure to withstand the movement and the changes caused by shifting ground—whether in small ways or as a result of a huge earthquake.

In addition to flexibility and strength, living from a place of curiosity is essential to begin living the Middle Way. Being able to say, "I don't know" is the Middle Way. It allows for the buffer of investigation. It allows me to gather information. It allows for the strength of respect for myself and others. Most especially, "I don't know" allows for flexibility. It means I'm going to let the pendulum swing. It allows for balancing things out. It means I'm going to allow for the space to see how I feel in this moment—in the now—asking questions such as: *What is really important for me in this moment? Am I peaceful? Am I joyful? Am I feeling respectful of myself and of you? Am I acknowledging my responsibility in this moment? Am I acknowledging my instinct without denying it or trying to control it?*

Every rose is different. Each one has a different smell, a different texture, a different color. No two roses are the same. Neither are any two people. So no two Middle Ways can ever be the same. As we consider our Middle Way and its evolution, it's important that we look at our judgments of right and wrong and become more interested in being joyful and peaceful rather than being normal or conforming. So the test of our *true* Middle Way must be that it is peaceful, joyful, and respectful.

11

LOVE, COMPASSION, AND RESPECT

AS WE TALKED ABOUT in Part One, a big piece of the conditioning we receive from our earliest beginnings is related to trying to fix ourselves in order that we can become perfect. We are conditioned to believe we are imperfect, flawed, and inadequate. We are taught to be self-critical and self-judging. Anything other than self-denigration can be considered vain and selfish. We are conditioned to focus on changing things externally, rather than going inward and looking at our internal landscape. Most people's lives are therefore built around this external struggle to achieve perfection, a goal that is absolutely unachievable.

We are also programmed through our upbringing, society, and our spiritual and religious traditions to be self-sacrificing and self-denying. We are conditioned to believe that only by serving others will we become better people. Self-sacrifice and self-denial are a part of what we're taught to do in order to work towards our perfection. This conditioning runs deep—it is cultural, societal, and generational—and we don't know anything better than this as we grow up.

This makes it almost impossible for us to have love, compassion, and respect *for ourselves*, even though love, compassion, and self-respect are primordial. We are trained to have love, compassion, and respect for something or someone externally—but not for ourselves. We are taught to care about family members, the people we love, a movement we believe in, or a cause we support. We put time and energy into those things because it feels like a good investment. When we do this to an extreme, though, we create incredible processes of pain within ourselves—perpetuating our patterns of self-sacrifice and self-denial.

It's easy to see how we get into this behavior. When we look at it more closely, we can see how normal it is to buy into acting this way because it is condoned and fostered by our society. It is reinforced externally and it is a part of our internal makeup. It is recorded in our DNA. We are wired genetically to focus on the external. Unfortunately, if we try to live with our focus only on the external, it is not sustainable.

For example, let's say I'm working with an institution that's against the abuse of animals, which is a very worthy cause, but I take it so far that I don't see how I'm harming myself. My ego doesn't see what I'm doing to myself when I'm devoting all my time to this cause. Imagine that I'm so involved with my role to help abused animals, that I completely disregard the rest of my life. Imagine that I put so much energy into the work I'm doing to stop animal abuse that I don't have time to talk to my daughter or time or energy to check in with my own family. I can take things so far in my efforts to help this cause that I also deny myself, so much so that I don't sleep, I don't eat, and I don't take care of myself physically. Imagine for a moment that I am like a cell in a body that puts all of its energy into fixing another group of cells. In the process of directing the cell's energy outward, it begins to deplete itself to the point that it can—and most likely will—die.

This is how diseases take hold in a person's body, and this is what we do with our lives and with our own bodies. We are like the individual cells that focus our energy externally to help other cells. We do this to the point of our own exhaustion, to the point that we deny where we are needed in our own lives. We do all of this to help others and yet we ignore what's happening closest to us. Then maybe something happens in our personal life—maybe we find out our child is in some kind of trouble or our spouse wants to leave us or we become sick—and we ask why. We wonder how ∞, which is supposed to be all about love and compassion, can do this to us. We get mad at life. We question the fairness of the situation. How is it possible, when we've been doing good works, when we've been working so hard to help others and giving so much of ourselves and our time, that now something is broken in our own family or our own body? How could that have happened?

We don't connect the dots. We don't see how we denied ourselves and our loved ones. We don't understand that we must first take care of ourselves before we reach out further. Just like the cell is responsible for itself, we must first be responsible for taking care of ourselves. And that means going inward.

Every spiritual practice is an invitation to go inward, not to focus outward. There is a reason ∞ created us so that we cannot see our own face, except through a reflection. Being able to see our face directly would be a huge distraction. It would prevent us from ever looking inward. Yes, we are able to see other people, but if we want to be the best we can be—not perfect, but the best we are capable of becoming—we have to look inside ourselves, not at the external.

Understandably, when we don't have love, compassion, and respect for ourselves, it's impossible to give it to someone else. Yet, that's what we try to do over and over again—we try to give to others what we are incapable of giving to ourselves. The result is the same as if we're overdrawing our bank account—we get over-extended. If my bank account is empty and I continue to use my debit card, I'll end up with all kinds of fees for being overdrawn. When my account is empty, I really can't pay for anything—whether that's food, or bills, or my daughter's college tuition. We understand the concept of over-extending ourselves financially. So why then is it so difficult to see that if we don't have love and compassion and respect for ourselves, we won't be able to have it to give to someone else?

When what we offer to another is false—when it's not present within ourselves—it honestly doesn't feel good. We feel exhausted and depleted. Our efforts hurt. It's tiring and frustrating. We get angry, resentful even, maybe ultimately telling the person that we're done with them and that we give up. We express our anger and frustration at the very same person we offered to support.

If our supply of money starts to run out, we can use a credit card to sustain ourselves for a while. Using credit might look like it's working to give us what we need, but eventually we'll end up in a worse place financially than when we started out, usually because we've maxed out our card and we're left with a lot of debt to manage. Similarly, when we offer this false support to someone else, something will eventually break down—whether it is related to our physical body or our emotional state, or it shows up in some other way that hurts us. It can be an illness or some other kind of suffering that we manifest, such as the breakdown of significant relationships in our lives. All of these manifestations are messages to us saying, "You don't really have the money! You're tapped out! You don't have anything to give!" We can ignore the messages and let things get even worse. Or we can listen, acknowledging that the messages are an invitation from ∞ to realize that if we want to donate the money, we have to save the money first.

How do we start to save? How do we begin to have love, compassion, and respect for ourselves? The best way is by removing ourselves from situations that deplete us—distancing ourselves from the energy and dynamics of those situations until we can build and give ourselves what we need. Otherwise, we risk reacting automatically in those situations. Once we see that we are depleted or frustrated or angry, we need to take some time for silence and introspection. It's important to give ourselves some space away from the situation in order to get a different perspective and see what we need as well as what we are doing. When we take that responsibility, we can see that we need to stop and take some time for ourselves.

We don't want to stay in a relationship that is hurting us, because we can end up hating ourselves as well as the other person. Imagine staying in a relationship and trying to deal with it even though we're suffering physically, mentally, and emotionally. First, we might say and do things to the other person that hurts them, and then, in response, they most likely will say and do something to throw back that hurt at us. It's the perfect chemistry that creates an explosion. And that explosion injures both parties.

It's important for us to understand the potential danger in any relationship—as well as the potential harm that can be done to both people as a result of getting stuck in an unhealthy situation. When we don't take ourselves away, we can get to the point that we start blaming everything and everyone that is external. It's easier to blame ∞, to blame life, to blame others—even though it's the way we're interacting with life that is the real problem.

I'm not criticizing what we usually do when we get depleted or threatened. I'm not saying that people should change and never react towards one another. That self-defense mechanism might save us when an intruder comes into our house and threatens our safety. But if you want to show love and compassion and respect for yourself *and* the other person, you need to remove yourself from the situation rather than ask them to change or criticize and ridicule them for their actions. Removing yourself and creating distance from a painful relationship is the behavior that demonstrates love, compassion, and respect for both people's humanity.

The ego that is responsible for our defense mechanisms works exactly like radar. The ego is always scanning outside because it wants you to see the external issue rather than any-thing that is internal. When we direct *all* the love, compassion, and empathy that we feel towards others—and none towards ourselves—we suffer. When we are able to put some of this energy that we put into fixing others into checking in on ourselves, we will feel completely different.

As I've talked about earlier, we need our egos. They are important and necessary to our survival. So the only way for us to fall in love with this mechanism that is the ego is to see it for what it is and to understand how powerful it is. It is an instinctive, protective mechanism that we all possess. We need to deeply understand that the ego is not a bad thing, and acknowledging how our egos operate doesn't mean there is anything that needs to be fixed. It does mean that we must respect our egos, acknowledging their beauty and benefits. Then we can begin to work with the ego, using love and compassion, as well as respect.

Practicing love, compassion, and self-respect for ourselves and someone else can sometimes feel uncomfortable and not necessarily look loving, at least according to what we've been programmed to believe is love. In order to truly show love, compassion, and respect for ourselves and others, there are times when we have to take actions that don't conform to our conditioning—and they can feel like the opposite of love to everyone involved. For instance, when a parent has to ask a teenager or an adult child to leave their home because of their behavior, the child can feel unloved and unwanted. The parent might feel guilty for needing to ask the child to leave. Outside friends and relatives might even question what the parent is doing and why. Others might accuse the parent of not really loving their child. The reality, though, may be that in order to take the most loving, compassionate, and respectful action, the parent has to ask the child to leave. That action may be what is necessary for the health and well-being of everyone involved.

The more we can create space—a buffer—that allows us to consider our actions in terms of love, compassion, and respect, the more likely our actions will truly come from that place and be the best for everyone involved, but most especially ourselves. As we talked about in the previous chapter, our Middle Way will not look like anyone else's—and, therefore, everyone may not be able to understand what we are doing or our motives. In each situation, the more we feel joy and peace as a result of our actions, the more likely it is that our actions have come from a space of love, compassion, and respect.

Sometimes, as we act from love, compassion, and respect, we have to face what we've done in the past that may have caused harm to ourselves and others. Our previous actions that were motivated by patterns, programming, and conditioning—that may have been a result of automatic defense mechanisms—can leave a trail of suffering and pain. This is where self-forgiveness comes in.

12

FORGIVENESS

WHAT EXACTLY IS FORGIVENESS and why is forgiveness important? To answer these questions, let's consider another one: Can you imagine how much forgiveness I need to have for myself when I realize what I've done in a situation to hurt someone else, when I understand that I didn't know what I was doing and that it wasn't about the other person at all? I need to be able to forgive myself for what I've done in the situation. So, the most important forgiveness is what I offer to myself. Once I understand that it is about me instead of the other person, that I made the mistake, and that I didn't know what I was doing at the time, I need to be able to forgive myself for what has happened.

Let me give you an example. One of my Buddhist teachers, who I loved deeply, was someone I had admired for months and months as I worked with him. One day I asked him, "What did you do before becoming a monk?" "I was a tiger hunter," he replied. I remember responding, "What? But I love tigers! How *could* you have done that?" Before I met him, I'd sent money to tiger organizations. So, here in front of me was this man, whom I loved and admired, who had been a part of helping in the destruction of the tiger species. Then he did something exactly as a small child does when they've made a mistake. He told me, "Felix, I didn't know." And I had the exact same feeling in response to those words as when a small child says, "I didn't know." With that "I didn't know," the energy of, "Why? How could you do such a thing?" was destroyed within me. My teacher's "I didn't know" was as innocent as the "I didn't know" of a child. And in response to what he told me, I felt forgiveness.

When I am able to forgive another, it's usually because I have been able to forgive myself for something that I didn't know in the past—moments when I've made mistakes and I didn't know what I was doing at the time. When we didn't know that what we were doing was a mistake, how can we or anyone else come to us and ask "Why?" or "How?" or "How could you?" Only a big ego would attempt to judge someone else's innocence.

So, it takes love and compassion to understand this innocence, this "I didn't know," rather than allowing the ego to judge you. The ego is the only one that judges. Your heart is never judging—your heart is embracing. How do I know when I put my heart out? Because I am able to say "I didn't know." And then I allow the love of ∞ to go through me to love myself and see who I am, to see the mistake and forgive myself, and to ask for forgiveness. With my heart, I am able to see with love and compassion what I did and what I didn't know.

Forgiveness is the result of me practicing love and compassion for me and you. It's what comes after the equal sign. Forgiveness is only possible when we add in love and compassion. ∞ wants you to fall in love with reality and forgive yourself and everyone else who hurts you—this is what ∞ cares about. This is what you are here to learn. ∞ invites us to use this practice with others as well as ourselves. When we believe we've been hurt or harmed, we are invited to contemplate the statement, "They didn't know," in order to allow for the possibility of seeing their actions from a different perspective—one that is more compassionate and loving.

If you don't have love and compassion, there cannot be forgiveness. We cannot just say, "I forgive." We cannot have another person just say, "I forgive." There must be love, compassion, understanding, and respect in order to have true forgiveness. It is like a salad or a smoothie—several separate things are required to act together in order to make a new whole.

Forgiveness is the result of falling in love with truth. You can only do that when you have a beautiful communion with what truth is. Maybe someone in a relationship throws things when they get mad. This seems bad, but what if we look at it from another perspective? What if that person who throws things can also be a protector and that person's family can be safe with them in the house. That perspective can be dualistic—it's relative. There are some things that we like and some things we don't like—that is true. It's true that someone throwing things can hurt. But what do we do? Do we fight with that reality or embrace that reality and surrender to it? Surrendering and being able to forgive are the most beautiful things in the world to do.

For me to forgive another person, I need to surrender my own ideas and beliefs, which is where the fire of pain actually begins. And that is the reason true forgiveness is so difficult. The ego doesn't like surrendering, because it loses its identity, its power, its control, its beliefs, and its ways of behaving.

I like to use the example of the lion. A lion is a lion and it behaves in certain ways because it is a lion. So am I going to fight and try to get the lion not to kill because I believe it is bad for the lion to kill? What will happen when I don't want to believe in the lion's true nature? I suffer by believing that I can change the lion's behavior, and when I'm not able to change the lion, I say it's the lion's fault that it kills.

The most difficult thing to do is to acknowledge what is, to acknowledge the truth of a situation. The lion is a lion, not a kitten, even though it might look like a kitten. If I respect the lion, I'm not going to get too close because I understand the truth that I could lose my life. That's the boundary. If someone throws things when they are angry, we don't have to get too close to them when they are upset. When we understand the person's nature and behavior, we can decide how much time we will spend with that person, under what circumstances, and what physical distance we need from them. Again, that's the boundary. When I know the truth of what is, when I understand the nature of what is, then I can begin to create a space, a silence, where I can be selective about what I really want to do and feel. The space allows me to see if it's more important to feel right or more important to be peaceful.

There's a moment of priorities. There's a moment when I have to choose between the two ways: either I want to be right and believe that what I believe is true—and then I'll feel really good—or I want to be peaceful. That's basically the difference between heaven and hell. The more that I am able to have love, compassion, and respect for the lion and the nature of the lion, the more peace I will feel. I can either try to tame the lion, which is me deciding I want to be right and feel really good about my power and abilities, or if I want to be peaceful and allow the lion to be the lion, I can create the space necessary for me to be safe, for me to be me, and for me to be at peace.

The choice to be peaceful is me getting closer to my higher self rather than trying to react and control. The choice is always here in the present moment. That's the gift that the present moment gives to you—the moment when you can decide who you are and what you will do. What happens when I know I have the choice? What happens when I begin to understand that the present moment is the only moment I have, when I get to choose if I want to suffer or be at peace?

Ultimately, what do I have to forgive in any situation or circumstance? Absolutely nothing, really. There is nothing to forgive when I bring in love and compassion, and truth. This nothingness is the most beautiful thing that a human can experience—it is heaven. This special moment, this space where the "I am" is *not*—where my ideas and what I know are *not*—is peace. And that peace knows how to observe and acknowledge. It doesn't know how to judge or like or dislike or cling. When we judge or cling, it's our minds acting. This peace comes from our hearts. Peaceful hearts embrace, acknowledge, and see the truth clearly. When we get to this point of choosing peace, there is no more need for forgiveness. There is nothing to forgive. The innocence, the respect, the love and compassion are all that is.

13

THE RECIPE FOR PEACE AND JOY

WHAT WE'VE BEEN looking at in this section are some of the essential ingredients for a spiritual life. Spirituality is not something outside of our everyday lives. When we live as a spiritual being, our spirituality is infused into every aspect of our life, down to the most mundane things we do each day. With the ingredients we've been talking about, we can create a recipe that produces a rich and flavorful life. These ingredients, when combined with other elements and when prepared mindfully, transform our lives and invite us to live with peace and joy in every moment.

Let's take a look at what we need to get started. To create a recipe for living peacefully and joyfully in the present moment, we have to begin with a little curiosity mixed with a certain amount of maturity. That maturity has nothing to do with a person's age—it has nothing to do with chronology.

I believe it has much more to do with karmic reincarnation, being polished over and over through each life we live until we get to the place where we are ready to embrace the truth of life.

Our intention to develop a recipe that creates peace and joy is not enough. We need to be conscious of what we are doing. We need to be mindful of the ingredients including their qualities, the amounts, how they interact, and the order in which they are added. We need to be aware of the potential chemical reactions of what we add. For instance, we know that if we add oxygen to fire, the fire will expand. We might even cause an explosion.

The final consideration is that the amounts, qualities of the ingredients, and order in which we add them will be different for each of us. There are a few basic ingredients for everyone, but each person's recipe will turn out to be unique to him or her. As a teacher, I'd love to be able to tell each of my students, "Come here and spend a month with me, do what I do, and you will find peace and joy." Unfortunately, that would be extremely disrespectful. Once again, it is about creating a recipe that represents each individual's Middle Way. I cannot tell someone else how to find their Middle Way or what they need for their Middle Way. We each have to find our own. As Buddha said, "Don't believe in anything I said." We each have to find our recipe on our own, because it is based on our individual experience. I can point things out, offer ideas about this recipe, but ultimately you'll have to try it for yourself. And that's why we need our curiosity and maturity to guide us along the way.

As we begin to create this recipe, the first thing we need is a pot. Remember, the pot is the container. It is not the "soup" we are creating. It needs to be clean and it needs to be ready to receive—to be the receptacle of what we are putting together. The pot is like our bodies—a very defined space, with limits for how much it is capable of enduring. So, what we put in cannot consist of properties that could potentially destroy the pot.

The first ingredient we need to put in is water—clean, clear water. Why? Because that clean, clear water is neutral. It allows us to put in the flavors and spices we want to enhance our unique recipe. It is like the silence needed by a musician to compose a song. Or the blank, white canvas needed by an artist to create a painting. It is very important to start with this neutrality. This clear, clean water is *something*. Although it seems as if it is nothing in its neutral state, it is essential to the creation of our soup. Because of its neutrality, it offers the potential to make the soup more than any of the ingredients could ever be on their own.

It feels to me as if this water, this liquid, is life itself. So, we ask ourselves, "How do I want to have this life? How do I want it to taste? Do I want my soup thick or thin? Vegetarian? Pureed or chunky?" That clear base allows us to create our soup in any flavor and consistency we want. The clear base also allows us to see what we are adding. If we drop a diamond into the water and the water is clear, we will be able to find it easily. However, if the water is muddy or murky, we won't be able to see the diamond and we could potentially lose it. The clear base not only lets us see exactly what we are adding, but how the ingredients are being integrated.

We also need that water to be uncontaminated. Even if the water is clear, there can be organisms in the water that we cannot see. If the water is contaminated, it will affect the outcome of the soup, so—just as we want to be as mindful as possible in each moment—we want to make sure the water is as pure as it can be.

Next, we want to add ingredients that will nourish and support us. We don't want to add ingredients that hold no value for us. For instance, just because your mother always added a hambone to her soup, if you are a vegetarian you won't want to add that to yours. Likewise, we want to avoid adding our past conditioning to this liquid that is life. That conditioning is like adding a condiment to the soup, so we want to be conscious about adding condiments that will create the flavor we are seeking. Opinions, judgments, and conditioning may create a soup that is bitter or extremely sour, and most likely that is not the flavor any of us want to taste.

The condiments and spices we add will be unique to each of us, even unique to when and where we create our soup. For instance, I may add South American cilantro to my soup because I know it has a very intense flavor. When I cook with South American cilantro, I know I only need one cup. However, if I cannot get South American cilantro and need to use American cilantro, I know I have to add three cups to get the same flavor and intensity. If I've had an upset stomach recently, I'll use less cilantro no matter which kind I have available. These spices are like the filters we each have—the lenses we look through at any particular moment. Those filters can change from day to day, so the spices may need to be adjusted based on where we are at that moment in time.

And that leads to one of the most important elements of all for us to consider in creating our soup—acknowledging where we are in this particular moment. Where we are is always *now*. It may be difficult to create a soup using Mexican spices when we are in Greece. We need to be able to adjust our ingredients based on where we are, and this requires flexibility. Allowing for the when and where of now will create something completely new—which may turn out to be more beautiful, more enjoyable, and even tastier than what we started out to create. Imagine if you stopped creating the soup because you couldn't find the exact ingredients you usually cook with—you will have missed out on an incredible experience. And if you have the expectation that your soup must taste the same as it would with Mexican spices, even if you have to use different spices from Greece, you're already muddying your soup. This is why it is so important to be conscious of what ingredients you are adding, what elements you are working with, and where you are in the here and now.

Just like what happens with expectations, your head may want to get into the game in other ways, bringing in all kinds of ideas about what needs to get added to the pot as you prepare your soup. Your head may want to add ingredients based on the past, without any regard for who and where you are at present. It may want to rush the process without any regard for the ingredients themselves, the amounts, the order, or how long they take to cook. If you are consciously creating your recipe, you'll be able to observe the intent of your head and tell it, "No thank you."

Creating this recipe is a deeply conscious experience. It requires that you be mindful of what you add to the soup, which is a very different way of approaching any recipe. It requires that you consider where you are in the present moment and the ingredients your mind wants to add based on your past experience. It requires that you learn from your past and be willing to consciously experiment each time you create the soup, based on each present moment and not on what worked or did not work in the past. Some batches of soup that you create may not taste good. Those batches, however, are not mistakes—they are a part of the process of experimentation, of EVOLUTION. Life itself is experimentation. And this is precisely why each person's recipe will turn out a bit different from every other person's and why each batch we create will be different from the previous one. For each new "present moment," for each new situation, what we create will be different and unique.

In allowing for the conscious creation of your recipe, you will end up with a soup that fills you with peace and joy. In the next part of this book, we will take a look at some of the elements that lead to conscious creation.

PART FOUR

Becoming the Observer

14

BECOMING CONSCIOUS

SITTING IN SILENCE each day in the monastery, as my teacher instructed me to do, something curious began to happen. Somehow in the silence I began to see that when I was concentrating on what I was doing in the moment I felt a beautiful sense of peace. But every time I went to the past or future, I felt a different sensation. When I would begin to believe the thoughts running through my head, I'd experience feelings connected to those thoughts. Sometimes I'd become unhappy or anxious or angry. And if I focused on what my body was feeling, I experienced other sensations. Sometimes it was a pain in my body, at other times it was hunger. When I felt sensations such as hunger, it took me to a feeling of the desire for food.

I began to experiment with the sensations I was feeling. For instance, sometimes I'd receive the signal mentally that said, "Go now! Get food now, because if you don't, you'll die. When you're hungry and don't eat, you'll die." The reality was that I would not die. A person can go a long time without food. But when I focused on the hunger or dizziness, I began to believe that if I didn't eat I'd faint. So, in my response to the message that I was hungry, I'd tell myself that I wouldn't die if I waited a little while before I ate. I began to extend the time and wait even longer. That waiting created a buffer between my thoughts and my actions.

The buffer gave me the opportunity to assess what was real. In that moment, I didn't die from starvation and I didn't faint. I was able to understand that the breakfast I'd eaten earlier could sustain me for days if necessary. So the trick I learned was not to deny that I was hungry or that I was having these sensations caused by my hunger, but to embrace the feelings and deeply understand them. Then, from that moment, from that space of clarity, I could continue to sit in silence without needing to eat immediately and without needing to stop my meditation. I acknowledged what my mind was telling me, and what I was feeling as a result of my mind's message, but then I was able to be in the space that the buffer created.

Ultimately, I saw that I had a choice in every moment. I could stay fixated on the past and all the bad things that had happened to me, worry about what I was going to do next and preoccupy myself with whether or not I'd ever feel better, focus on my bodily sensations and get caught up in the worry of how to stop them, become anxious about what might happen to me—or I could allow myself to experience the space of expansiveness where I was completely immersed in the present moment and could assess what was real in that moment. I came to understand the power my mind could have over me when I believed my thoughts rather than what was real in each moment. And I came to see that the ultimate power was in that expansive space of the present moment, where I could experience peace and joy, and mental, physical, and psychological health.

We do not need to leave our homes or our families in order to seek understanding and to learn to become conscious in every moment. It is necessary, though, for human beings to take a little time to consider questions such as: Why am I suffering like this? Why am I getting sick? Why am I dealing with this stress? Why aren't I happy? Why do I feel empty? Why does it feel as if something is missing from my life? In order to explore these thoughts, we need to step out of our daily routine and take some time alone. We can do that at any time during our day—for a few moments or a few hours.

In considering these questions, imagine a native living in the Amazon. How is that he is much healthier than most people living in metropolitan areas? He does not own a car, a television, a computer, a cell phone, or any of the other material items most of us possess. Yet, without possessing what most of us believe we must have to feel satisfied, he is much more joyful. Why is it that the native seems to have so much more peace than individuals who are living and working in urban and/or suburban areas? Quite simply, it is because he engages with and enjoys the moment. He appreciates the task at hand. He focuses on what is right in front of him. He does not have time for anything other than what he must do to provide for himself, his family, and his community. He learns from his mistakes, and he doesn't repeat them again. He is focused on now in order to survive.

Although as a society we also focus on caring for ourselves and others, we are burdened with thoughts of the past and future, with expectations, and with longing for what we do not have. These thoughts, and all they lead us to do, overload and overwhelm us. As a result, we deplete ourselves to the point that we sacrifice our health, our peace, and our joy. This is the fertile ground for illness and disease to take root.

The native in the Amazon uses his survival mechanisms to survive in the moment—to deal with real "present moment" dangers, while in our modern society, we abuse ourselves by overusing our survival mechanisms and imagination in situations that our mind tells us are dangerous but are not actually real. The illnesses that the native deals with are usually not related to mental or psychological or emotional conditions—they are as a result of their interaction with their environment.

In our society, illness and disease are a big problem. Yet, these states are not natural for the body. The body's natural state is to heal itself, and the body knows how to do that. Every cell in your body is a healing organism. Your cells are programmed to multiply in a healthy way. Cells don't know anything else but to heal and be healthy. They are programmed to heal and they have that instruction in their memory. So how can we invite the cells to do what they know inherently? Understanding is needed—we must consider questions such as the ones I've listed above in order to begin to live in a healthier state. When we don't understand what is happening or why, we create internal fights within our bodies.

Our minds attempt to help us understand, because that's the work of the machine—to help us out. In an attempt to do that, the mind takes us to the past and the future. But those places are not real. What happened in the past is gone and what's going to happen in the future doesn't yet exist. I've discovered that the reason many people get sick is because they treat the past and future like hallucinations, imagining things and believing in the moment that they're real. We take ourselves on these bad trips, imagining things that don't really exist, yet engaging hormonally and emotionally as if they are real. Because our minds are wired to keep us alive and help us survive, they always take us to worst-case scenarios; the mind never takes us to best-case situations. But the body doesn't know what's real—the body cannot differentiate. The body is designed to follow the thoughts that are happening in the mind in the moment.

Here is a somewhat funny example ... what exactly is a wet dream in a young man? The person is imagining something and the body gets totally engaged. In this case, the mind triggers an organ and the organ produces a certain hormone. In this scenario, the hormone is testosterone. The body, if it's a healthy body, feels in a certain way and is totally responsive. But where is the girl in this example? The body doesn't know if the girl is real or not and that's why it becomes totally engaged with the scenario. The body doesn't need to know if she's real in order to be engaged and respond.

In the same way testosterone triggers certain responses, adrenaline, cortisol, and norepinephrine trigger breakdowns in the body. Stress hormone breakdowns happen with stress. When we are stressed out, we experience a rush of all three. The wet dream scenario is fun, but the ones I'm interested in when I work with people are not so funny because they can create diseases and unnecessary suffering.

How we deplete the cells, even in an organ that is completely healthy, is by leaving the present and going into thinking about the past, the future, the whys, the hows, and the what ifs. The stress hormones and chemicals that come with leaving the present moment are as strong as heavy drugs. Since we don't see them, we can trick ourselves into believing that these stress hormones and chemicals are harmless. When someone is using drugs, such as cocaine or heroin, it's easy for us to see those as potentially harmful. We may even say something like, "Wow! That is strong stuff. That person could have a heart attack."

Believe it or not, you can drink a whole bottle of vodka and feel horrible afterwards, but it's difficult to be killed by it. Shot-up stress hormones, however, can give you a heart attack. Unfortunately, we are not taught to see how powerful these internal chemicals are—the ones pumping through our bodies even if we are not smoking or drinking anything. As I work with people, I allow them to see how powerful stress hormones and chemicals are, how they are produced, and how dangerous they can become over time.

In order to be aware of what kind of chemistry we are creating in our bodies, we must be conscious and responsible. We must develop a deep communion within by respecting ourselves—all parts of us, including our minds. In an attempt to help us, our minds take us to what has happened previously to the body. Most of the time, our minds take us to what was painful. It does this to keep us safe and avoid future pain. As we become more aware of how our minds work, it's important that we don't try to negate our minds. With love and compassion, it's important to remember that our minds are necessary for our survival. Our mind is there to judge and assess in order to keep us safe.

I see people get mad at their minds, mostly people searching for spirituality, saying things like, "Oh, I hate my mind!" But we need the mind—it is programmed to keep us alive. Our mind gets activated through fear, and the ultimate fear is of dying. My invitation to you is to treat your mind with curiosity, love, and compassion and see how relaxed you can begin to feel.

If you attack your mind, the part of you that is the master of survival, it's going to respond—it may even attack you. Remember that the nature of the mind is to respond to help you. How many times do we use our mind in ways that don't really serve us, either by overusing it or ignoring it? I see the mind like a big cat. I see it with that majestic beauty—I love it but I'm not going to fight it because it's a matter of time before I'm going to get hurt by it. The mind is a very big, strong force. Your mind is a machine that was given to you and designed by ∞ to help you survive, and it's not going to do anything other than that. So it's going to endure.

If I try to make my mind quiet (another thing I hear people say is, "I'm going to make my mind completely quiet"), my efforts will be unsuccessful. This is why not many people like meditation. When you attempt to quiet your mind, you strain yourself, trying to stop something that cannot be stopped. I invite you to, as much as possible, stop trying to fight this lion. Maybe you can then even begin to have fun with it.

It's also important to understand how the mind judges. It judges and assesses to be able to survive. If it sees fire, for instance, it judges the fire as something dangerous. Then, as an attempt to help you avoid pain and the possibility of death, it creates a certain response. It assesses whether you need to run away or distance yourself from it.

It's a beautiful thing that the mind judges, but what usually happens is we overuse our minds. It's good to judge the fire. Or a food that is too spicy for me—it's good to judge that food and say it's too spicy in order to decide I'm not going to eat it for my well-being and comfort. But what we usually do with our minds is begin to over-judge everything, including friendships, relationships, and most especially ourselves. This creates the sea of suffering within us that the Buddha talked about.

The challenge becomes how to acknowledge the mind without engaging it automatically and instantly. The opportunity for every person is to learn to take what the mind offers without allowing it to overrun us or the situation. Again, this takes conscious and mindful living, which requires awareness and practice. Becoming mindful is a simple concept, but the practice of it is not easy. Let's take a look at why that is so.

15

THE MIND AS A TOOL

THE BRAIN AND THE MIND are two separate entities that work together as one. The brain is like a computer. It's the hardware and the mind is the software inside the computer. These two were given to us to be used together as a tool, and that tool is intended to help us do one thing—survive. Everything that the hardware and software do together is intended to help us stay alive. In attempting to do that, the mechanism often takes control of us—our thoughts, our actions, our reactions, and the way we feel. When that happens, it no longer operates like a tool to support us. Our goal is to learn to use the mind as a tool rather than to allow the apparatus to control everything we do, think, and automatically feel. The problem begins when we allow the apparatus to take over—this is where the trouble starts and what leads us into suffering. As with any other tool, we have to learn how to use it carefully;

otherwise, the tool can harm us. The mind has to be trained to serve us, not for us to serve our minds.

The typical human being follows the mind and believes automatically every thought that is running in the software. We identify with these messages of the mind as if they are our whole reality, as if they are the TRUTH. We say things like, "I am hungry," or "I am insecure," as if this is *all* we are. We put the thought in our head as if that is really happening, and yet many times, that is not true. What I believe as the truth is what creates the feeling.

Because of the way we live, we overuse this mechanism— this machine. We are conditioned to do so. Even though primitive man seems really far away from us and the way we live today, we still have the same fears as these ancestral primates. We have basic fears of survival, such as whether or not we'll have enough food or a house where we can take shelter. We seek security—a security, by the way, that is unreal. Because what does it mean to be secure? You can have a house, you can have adequate food to eat, but you still can't know what might happen tomorrow.

What I strive to teach people is to learn how to live with this machine that we have in our heads and use it in ways that serve them, acknowledging that we all have our programs— and some of them we don't even like. The fact that we each have our programs means that the mind is working perfectly. It is doing what it is supposed to do. The question becomes whether or not we have to listen to the mind all the time.

Let me give you an example. I am a vegetarian. Sometimes I walk in front of a fast-food hamburger place and it triggers a response in me. I know I won't eat a hamburger, but still my mind gives me the invitation, "Wow, this is going to be really pleasurable to have a hamburger! It's been so long!" I need to understand that I am not messed up in my head for having this thought. My mind is simply going back to a past time when I did eat hamburgers as a young person. Because it was pleasurable for me back then, my mind is offering the invitation to experience it once more. Rather than get angry or frustrated, I can pause and remember why I no longer eat hamburgers. Once I consider that information, I can then make my final decision not to eat one—without feeling angry or guilty or shameful for having considered the invitation in the first place.

This is what I hope to cultivate in others—the ability to have a practice where each of us is more conscious of our minds' process as we consider the actions we will take. Those actions are what will create our reality—in the present moment. Then, each of us can live more joyfully. When we don't have to fight with our heads, we can develop a communion with our deep wisdom and understand how our minds work, being able to be more in charge of what our minds tell us to do.

We want the end result of our consciousness to be that our actions are balanced and serve us. For one person, it might be taking a yoga class once in a while. For another person, it might be attending yoga a couple times each week. For another, it might be practicing yoga daily. And for someone else, it might be to never even try it. As we discussed before, we each have to find our Middle Way.

To get there, we have to learn to use a practice that allows for space between the impulse and our decision. I refer to that practice as "acknowledging the signal." In the example of me contemplating a hamburger, I first acknowledge the impulse, "Here is me wanting to have a burger. Of course, because my belly feels hungry and I am standing in front of a fast-food hamburger restaurant, I understand the reason that I am having this thought." In making my decision of what action I will take, the decision needs to come from my conscious thought rather than the instinctual animal response. Remember, the one wanting to have the burger is the animal who is hungry. It is the conditioned animal machine that was established when I was young and ate hamburgers. It remembers that eating a hamburger was the way to stop hunger.

I can acknowledge that the animalistic machine is working perfectly; however, I don't need to engage with that machine. I only engage with it if the result of the suggested action will make me feel joy. Now, I may recall another memory of eating a hamburger more recently and feeling like a stone was sitting in my belly. The mind remembers. The body may even feel the experience as I think back to that time. So I remember the past experience, recall what I learned from that particular event, and then decide I do not want to repeat the way I felt. The process has worked perfectly, helping me remember what happened previously. The experience I recall was not a mistake; rather it was an event that taught me something. Now, I can put what I learned to use and not eat a hamburger. By acknowledging the signal and allowing time for more recollection, I am able to come to a decision that is conscious and brings joy and a sense of peace. I also have a sense of gratitude to my body for offering the information about how I felt the last time I ate a hamburger.

Rather than judge myself or beat myself up or become angry because I "almost ate another hamburger," I can feel grateful for the information I received. That kind of judgment never serves us. However, the judgment that comes from assessment and evaluation is helpful. The type of assessment that is not going to make me feel bad, but instead is going to help me stop a behavior or a pattern that is harmful to me in my life, is worth it. Any kind of judgment comes from the mind. Yet, when we make an assessment, we involve the heart. The assessment is almost like an observation. When I recall how the hamburger felt in my stomach, I observe it with my heart. I have compassion for how I felt then and for how I'll feel now if I eat the burger. There is nothing to feel good or bad about. By involving the heart and assessing with the deepest part of me, I can recognize that the hamburger will not serve me or my hunger. Because I bring compassion into the process, it is not possible for me to feel bad about my thoughts.

We need to train our minds to listen to what the deepest part of us is saying and to execute what comes as a result of that information. It is not the mind's job to tell us what to do. The mind is there to give certain information, such as when our stomach feels empty and in need of food. That information is helpful and can be really useful. That information is not, however, good or bad.

The mind machine works by going to the past or future. In the example of the hamburger, the information from the past can help me to make a decision that will serve me best in the present. When I consider how my stomach felt after I ate a hamburger the last time, I can then ask myself, "Is it worth it?" If it is worth it and it will serve me to eat the hamburger, then it's important for me to do so. If I decide it is not worth it because of the pain I experienced previously, then I will choose not to eat it. Even though it may feel pleasurable and satisfy my need for instant gratification to consume the hamburger, the recollection of how I felt afterwards will keep me from eating it.

Every action has a consequence. So my actions should be followed with joy and a sense of peace. If I do not feel joy and peace as a result of my actions, then I am not doing what is best for me—what is for my highest good. It is not about good or bad; it is about what will serve me best. Being mindful means I am conscious of my choices as well as the reasons for my decisions and actions *in each and every moment*. Being mindful means I enter the space where I can connect with the deepest part of myself.

16

ENTERING THE SILENCE

WHETHER WE THINK we are or not, we are all always looking for inner silence. We are always seeking that vibration within ourselves that is the true us. This is the peace we all seek. We are always searching for it, yet because it is covered up with ideas and thoughts from our minds, it is almost impossible for us to believe that it actually exists. Our ideas, beliefs, conditioning, and assumptions cover up our ability to connect with that silence, that inner space. As hard as it may be to see, even in the midst of our very busy lives, our multiple "to do" lists, our creativity, and our striving for success, we are searching for that inner silence. Any time you hear that quiet voice telling you to stop or slow down or take a break, it is the search for silence in action. Yet, we don't honor that small voice most of the time. And when we don't, we feel stress and we suffer—sometimes we become ill in the process of pushing and striving to move forward.

Our minds are part of the reason we do not hear that small, quiet voice. Our minds do everything possible to keep the noise going. They do not like this inner silence. That silence, the inner stillness and inner peace, feels like death to the mind, so the mind has a problem with it and cannot accept it. Because the mind is here to help us survive, the mind doesn't like anything that seems to threaten our survival. Inner silence is a very big threat to the mind, since from the mind's perspective it may mean we have died.

When I am able to understand my mind's position, I do not need to have it agree with the silence. In fact, it is completely okay that the mind has a little issue with silence. If my eyes are open enough to see that my mind cannot deal with the silence, I won't fight my mind. I know that this issue has a place—it can actually be useful—so I allow my mind to have its position. I am not going to put too much focus on the issue; I am not going to fight my mind or deny it. Rather, I acknowledge and allow my mind its perspective, knowing that my mind is a part of me in the same way my arm is a part of me. And the great thing is that the less I actually focus on my mind and its issue, the less noisy my mind is. That allows me to tap into the inner silence.

We want to cultivate the search for and connection with that inner silence as much as possible. It feels to me that there are three ways to get to this place or to create the invitation to go there. The first is to sit and meditate, which we will talk more about in Part Four. The second is through activities that actually create a level of silence within us. Participating in sports is an activity that invites us into the silence. Any time we do something that requires us to be fully engaged, we actually tap into that silence. Without striving to get there, we enter the inner silence of the present moment. We may think we enjoy the activity because of the thrill we feel—for instance, while surfing or skiing—but I believe we are actually drawn to the *silence* that is created. Whether you are surfing, skiing, or biking, when you do these activities your mind needs a level of silence. When it doesn't have that silence, you can get hurt.

Let me give you an example. I remember seeing an interview with a professional driver. The interviewer asked him, "What are you thinking about when you are driving at 300 miles per hour?" The driver responded that he is not thinking about anything, because if he were to think about something while going at such a high speed, he could easily end up in the other dimension. Although the mind is completely engaged in the activity, the body identifies with the thrill. If you were to measure his stress hormones, his levels would be high. So a person doing something that contains an element of thrill believes that it is the adrenaline and the other stress hormones—the high—that he loves. Yes, these hormones are pumping—physically, it is happening. That physical reaction is actually needed. But in the reality of the experience, the mind is completely present, yet not thinking about anything else. The sport—this intense activity—actually forces the mind into a mindfulness practice.

I know a couple of people who went to the top of Mount Everest, and when I asked them what they were thinking about while they were climbing, they said they thought about nothing. They both made it to the summit of the mountain. They said that in order to keep walking, they could not think about anything. They felt that thinking about anything other than walking would be a waste of energy—a waste of calories. Imagine that! And it is true. Engagement with our minds can create wasted energy. So athletes, such as the climbers and the driver, even the surfer and the skier, go into what they call "the zone." The climbers walk in the zone. The driver drives very, very fast in the zone. The skier and the surfer are both doing what they're doing in the zone. As soon as they move out of the zone, they risk something going wrong. They risk being injured or even dying.

The third way we enter the silence is in nature. When you walk in a forest, you *feel* the environment. You don't try to make sense of anything. You don't analyze. You are not usually asking, "Why are there rocks on the ground? Why are there more trees to the left than the right of the path?" You experience your surroundings. You engage your senses. You become a part of the experience. As soon as you begin to explain, interpret, or think about what you are experiencing, you remove yourself from the experience—you become separate from it. For instance, as you watch a sunset or a sunrise, if you begin to think about the colors and the clouds and the position of the sun, you take yourself out of the experience. When you are able to *be* in nature, you are once more tapping into that inner silence contained in the present moment.

17

Cultivating Inner Peace

IN THE LAST CHAPTER we looked at some of the ways we can tap into the inner silence of the present moment. Cultivating inner peace starts with that inner silence. Nature and sports, and being thoroughly engaged in any activity, can take us there. Cleaning up the canvas of our lives is another way to get to the inner silence.

As I mentioned earlier, when an artist begins a new painting it's best to start with a white canvas. This allows the artist the freedom and flexibility to create whatever he desires. Unfortunately, as human beings, by the time we reach adulthood our inner canvases are filled with lots of colors and shapes. They are shaded and tinted by our past conditioning, our past experiences, our beliefs, our judgments, our assumptions, and our fears. Usually, when we go about making changes in our lives, we continue to layer more onto our already stained canvases and we don't even realize we're doing that. For instance, when we begin a new relationship, we think that everything about it is completely new. Yet, we come into that relationship with our stained canvas. Most likely, so does the other person. Before long, we see the same patterns repeating themselves. We may be in a new relationship, but we are still our same old selves.

I remember the first time I went to the Buddhist monastery. I told the monk, "I want to come as soon as possible. I want to get out of here." The monk responded, "Make sure you pull everything that's in the backpack out of the backpack; otherwise, you are going to be bringing basically your mess here with you, and I am not interested in your mess. Make sure you take care of it before you come." I remember having a second conversation with him. I said, "So here I am, I'm ready now," and he replied, "You are still carrying the backpack. It's a matter of time before you'll repeat the same behaviors. By nature, you are going to start putting the same things into that backpack again. Come back when you do not even have the backpack anymore." I remember being extremely mad. *Why is he saying that? Am I not good enough to be where he is? Why not? So I am not ready? Really?* My ego was really mad.

I felt I'd put in so much effort, yet he was rejecting me. His words really hurt. "But you still have the backpack full of stuff and I am not interested. And I don't think that you are interested in that stuff either. You will repeat your mistakes, but I believe you don't want to repeat them." At least what we repeat should be fun, and he was reminding me that some of the mistakes I'd made, if I did repeat them, would not be fun. They would probably harm me and others. Even though I believed I had cleared out my backpack and was ready to receive new things to put in there, he wanted me to get rid of the backpack completely. He wanted me to come to the monastery with a clean canvas. Otherwise, how would I ever have space for the new?

We have to clean up our inner canvases. We have to put our focus on seeing how clean they can become in order to reach that inner silence and place our attention into this silence. This inner silence actually helps us clean our inner canvases even more. The inner silence is the most beautiful place because it is uncreated. It is about to be created, but it is not yet created. The silence we are talking about is called "emptiness" in Zen Buddhism. In Hinduism it is netti netti. This silence, this nothingness, is the most powerful thing you can imagine. This nothingness is ∞ in creation. When it is created, this nothingness becomes somethingness.

Humans are the instruments that allow this nothingness to become somethingness, and it can only happen in the silence. Imagine the responsibility we have as humans. Unlike other animals—a cat, for instance, that functions at an entirely primal level—we have this bigger responsibility. All humans are invited to embrace it. We are the tool for ∞ to move through. This uncreated force is being created through us when we are *being* that instrument.

In order to be this conduit, it's essential that we are as uncluttered as possible. That is what we are doing through our spiritual practices—clearing and entering the silence in order that ∞ can be made manifest through us. This uncreated force is what Christians call God. The Buddhists call it Metta—the love and compassion that is inside your heart.

This pure incredible energy that goes through you like electricity traveling through a cable is ∞.

This is why it is essential that we—as the cable, the conduit—be clear about what is within us. Is there an obstruction? Is there something that does not allow the electricity to move through, something that stops the electricity? Is there something that taints and changes the properties of the electricity? The quality of the conduit is based on what is within the cable. The quality of the cable itself is based on what it is made from.

So there is always this search for quality in our spiritual practices—quality that is more in accord with who we are in the moment. That quality comes from the way we eat, the way we move, the way we talk, the people we have in our lives, and the way we engage with our thoughts. The quality is not based on how much money we make or spend. It is like the soup recipe we spoke about earlier. The quality of the spices, condiments, and ingredients will not be based on their price. Rather, it will be based on where we are, how and where the ingredients are grown, and what kinds of flavors we want to create to bring the results we desire. Just like the ingredients in the "soup" will be different for each of us, the qualities of the cable we create for the conduit through which ∞ passes will be unique to each of us.

What is essential to all human beings is that we find a way to get as close to this nothingness within ourselves as possible so the creative force that is not yet created can move through us—along with what is created, what was created, and what will be created. In that nothingness we feel peace. It is an immense power, yet it is like the tranquility and neutrality of water in a glass. Understanding the qualities of this nothingness is like looking at the water in a clear glass. The water looks like nothing. When that water has the right force, however, it can literally destroy an island. If there are microbes in that water, it has the potential to kill thousands of people in seconds. The nothingness of the water is immense and simultaneously powerful. This nothingness, this emptiness within us, is the same—it is inherently powerful and filled with potential.

Yet, in our culture, we see this nothingness like an empty box—and our mind views this emptiness as dangerous and weak. Our mind asks, "Okay, how am I going to survive with nothing if I do nothing?" This is how our mind tricks us. Our mind literally tells us we are being irresponsible. "How can you do nothing about *that?*" it asks when you choose to acknowledge a situation without taking some forceful action. "Okay, now you are going to play the game that you don't need me. Well, let's see what happens to you when you do not need me! Go ahead and do nothing and see what happens to you!" These are the kinds of messages our mind tells us when we choose not to act in the ways our families and society expect. Our minds trick us into thinking that this nothingness is like going hungry—as if we'll starve to death. But out of this nothingness actually comes an intense amount of energy for me to plan a meal and then eat it! This emptiness is everything. This everything that is nothing—and this nothing that is everything.

Because these concepts are very confusing for our minds, it's important to understand that these ideas of emptiness, nothingness, and everything are not going to be digested by our head very well. Again, our mind is going to have an issue with this idea of nothingness and emptiness because it sees them as synonymous with dying or being dead. So, I have to choose not to listen to my mind alone. My mind is not going to change its reason for existing—which is to keep me alive—so I don't have to deny it or resist it. I simply have to acknowledge it and thank it but not continue to listen to only my mind.

The gift of experiencing nothingness is peace and joy. In that nothingness of the inner silence, we are able to experience a blank canvas. In that space that is not tainted by our filters, or programmed by our conditioning, we experience freedom. In that emptiness, we are free from the lower-level us, from our conditioning, and from our beliefs. We are free from our assumptions and expectations. In that space, we are able to be ∞. We are perfection itself. Imagine what will happen when each of us discovers that today we are perfection itself. We are free to experience tremendous peace, joy, and congruence in this nothingness. And the best way to connect with this nothingness that is everything is through our mindfulness practices.

PART FIVE

THE INVITATION

The Beginning of Meditation

I SEE A LOT OF PEOPLE *trying* to meditate, and they are really good at trying but really bad at meditating. For me, meditating is that space where you acknowledge your thoughts but you do not engage with them. In the acknowledging, there is nothing for you to do. It's just like when you see a cloud—there is nothing for you to do. You acknowledge the cloud, but you don't try to move it faster or slower or further away or closer to you. You simply acknowledge that the cloud exists. You are not doing anything other than observing the cloud. In the same way that trying to move a cloud would be frustrating, and impossible, trying to stop thoughts is equally frustrating. It is also equally impossible.

When people come to me and say that meditation is not for them because they're not good at it, I soon learn that their practice consists of sitting and trying to stop their thoughts.

They try to stop their mind, which is impossible to do. If we have healthy minds, they are going to be active. That's a good thing for us. We need our minds to be active. Unfortunately, those active minds frustrate people when they try to meditate.

I remember my first teacher offered a kind of trick to me. "Okay, go and sit and see if you can stop your mind." And I was there for hours, basically wasting my time. Then he asked me, "So … what happened?"

And I replied, "Well, I was trying to stop my mind."

"Were you able to?"

"No."

"Okay, keep trying."

And, you know, it took months until I came to the conclusion that I could not do that. I could not stop my mind. Eventually, I understood deeply that it could not be done. So the next question was, "What do I do now?" And it was beautiful when I was able to see that I could allow my mind to do what it does best, but I did not have to engage with it. Instead of fighting my mind, I could allow it to be. That's when I began to have a totally different experience of meditation. This was the beginning of me being able to deeply understand my mind—my mind and its movements. It was as if I came to an agreement with it—I allowed it to do what it does best and it allowed me to meditate.

Remember, the mind exists to protect you and help you survive. So the more you fight your mind, the more it responds, and the louder and noisier it becomes. If you can leave it alone, without engaging in the thoughts it offers, you begin to have an experience of real meditation. Automatically, you begin to have the experience of silence. The more you allow your mind to have its own space and respect the mind's need for that space, the less the mind reacts. Eventually, the mind doesn't even bother you anymore. It becomes quieter. This is real meditation. This is the purest meditation.

There are many different kinds of meditation, and some of them are very beautiful. But most of them make you do something. They require that you breathe a certain way or count a certain way or see colors in a certain way. Some ask you to focus on the flame of a candle. Some ask you to pray and recite a mantra. Even praying the rosary can be a form of meditation. These can be very useful because each of these practices requires that you focus on just one thing. All of them are really powerful because they are teaching you to concentrate on one thing at a time, which, by the way, is the only thing that the mind really can do. These meditations take you closer to the silence but not into it.

What I see in all of these types of meditation is that they prepare you to go into a deeper meditation practice, one where you enter the silence, but they are *not* that practice. After a person has mastered any of these other forms of meditation, I always invite the individual to see what happens when they begin to practice in a deeper way. It can be very difficult for them, especially if someone has been practicing another form, such as a prayer or mantra, for a very long time. Because it has been working for them, they sometimes tell me, "You know, Felix, this makes me quiet. It relaxes me." I understand that this is true. What they have been doing does allow them to get quiet and relax. But I then tell them that there is a deeper level of relaxation available to them.

When someone uses a mantra or prayer, for example, they are still in the *somethingness*. This is not a bad thing—there is no good or bad in any of this. That prayer or mantra is effective and does relax the person. But I want them to discover that they can have a deeper meditation practice, one that does not engage with the mind. Although these practices allow a person to focus and become more relaxed, it is as if we are giving the mind a job, we are giving our minds something to do, which prevents us from entering the inner silence of *nothingness*. My invitation is always to go deeper.

19

Why Meditate?

WHEN PEOPLE ASK ME, "Why should I meditate?" I have many answers to that question. Let me share with you the one I believe is most significant of all.

One of the benefits of meditation is that your mind will not go to the past or future as often. By meditating more regularly, your energy—the energy of your body—is going to be able to feel where it belongs and where it is needed, even when you are not meditating. The more you meditate, the more your life becomes a living meditation. Your mind gets used to having your thoughts acknowledged without you needing to engage with them automatically. This creates a buffer within you that is always there, even when you are not meditating. So when something happens in your life that you would normally have an automatic emotional response to, you begin to go into the silence of that buffer—that space within—and choose how you will respond. The deeper your meditation practice, the deeper your ability to go into that silence in everyday life, the stronger that buffer becomes, and the longer it lasts.

As you become more selective with your responses, you begin to create a super human version of you. Why a super human? Because you are no longer acting like an animal and having an animalistic response to situations. You no longer act from your pain-body—your assumptions, conditioning, or your expectations—and this is extremely valuable. Going into that silence before reacting or responding to a situation that would have previously caused you to have an automatic reaction is the best means to avoid acting in a way that causes pain and suffering for all involved. As with your ability to acknowledge the thoughts of your mind when you meditate, you are able to acknowledge situations without reacting immediately, and that allows you to move and act in ways that serve you and others. In this silence created by the buffer, you can acknowledge everything that is happening. The power of this buffer is that you are then able to access your heart and tap into understanding, love, and compassion.

As a super human, you slow down your responses and respond consciously. As a super human, you develop a heart muscle that is stronger and manifests actions and responses that are for the highest good of everyone. The bigger YOU takes over—the you that is ∞.

20

THE CONTAINER OF SPIRITUALITY

JUST LIKE A POT IS NEEDED to hold soup when we prepare it, we have to remember that we are a container that holds the part of us that connects with ∞ as well as our ego mind. It is like we are a bottle that holds both water and oil. If the bottle is full and we want to add more oil, we'll need less water. If we want more water, we'll need to reduce the amount of oil. Because the bottle holds a finite amount of liquid, we have to choose how much of each we can pour in.

Let's say that the water is your consciousness, the deepest you that is learning through spiritual practices and strengthening your spirituality. Your spirituality deepens, getting stronger and more expansive. The inner silence that you are able to enter causes the water to increase. The amount of water grows as you are able to be more mindful in situations. So obviously the oil has to be reduced. The oil is the old, small you—your ego mind and the way you used to react automatically to the events and circumstances in your life.

If you decide that as you add to the bottle you still want to keep both liquids in there without reducing either, what is going to happen to the bottle and its contents? If there is no lid on the bottle, the liquid is going to overflow. If there is some kind of pressure, maybe because there is a lid on the bottle, the bottle will break. It will not be able to contain an amount greater than what it can hold.

This is basically what happens to us. Both our consciousness and our ego mind are contained within our body. If, as we grow spiritually, we decide we want to keep all our past conditioning and programming, our assumptions, our old stories, old patterns of behavior, even old patterns of pain, something has to give. Even though we may love certain aspects of who we thought we were, we will not be able to sustain the "HIGHER me" along with the "Little me" in the same amounts. Something has to happen, because these two energies cannot be sustained in a container that stays the same size.

Just like the bottle that breaks under the pressure of more liquid, something will happen to us to cause us to look at what we are doing. We will not be able to maintain the proportions. Maybe, like the bottle breaking, an organ will break down in our body—we'll have an internal reaction to trying to sustain these two energies in the same amounts. Or maybe like the liquid spilling over, something will happen to us externally. Maybe I'll get into an accident, maybe I'll end up in a wheelchair. In order to manifest who I really am, something will occur to invite me to be the HIGHER me in higher vibration.

Most of the time people understand that they cannot hold all of who they were as they grow spiritually. Sometimes, though, it takes time, experimentation, and opportunities to help us gain clarity. One day, after repeating an old automatic response, you may ask yourself, "Why am I repeating this again? Why am I talking like this? Why did I get into a relationship like this again when I said I was going to do something totally different?" With deep respect for the old behavior, with love and compassion for what you didn't understand previously, you might be able to answer, "Now I understand." This is the beginning of allowing more space for the water than the oil. This is the understanding that allows you to stop responding the same old way. This understanding creates a new priority within yourself, where something becomes more valuable than responding automatically. The practice of being and acting mindfully changes you. Your meditation practice that allows you to access the deeper **BIG YOU** changes everything. And as you and your responses are changed, so will others' responses be changed as well.

MOMENTS OF MINDFULNESS

AS EXPRESSED EARLIER, the practice of mindfulness is a very simple one. It is putting all of your energy and focus into the present moment, whatever the present moment is. Sometimes the present moment is filled with so much beauty or engages us so completely because of the activity we're involved in that we enter it without any resistance or objection from our mind, but at other times the present moment can be filled with people and events that make it hard to engage. Sometimes you might want to turn around and run.

Being present to someone who is threatening to take their life, for instance, may be difficult because of what it brings up in you. Not wanting to lose them from your life, you may choose to cajole and plead with them. If you have strong religious and moral conditioning, you may tell them they can't take their life because it would be a sin and they'll go straight to Hell. You may get so scared by what they're saying that you find yourself wanting to ask someone else to deal with it. If you once considered suicide yourself, you may go immediately back to your own memories. All of these responses, as we've talked about previously, are automatic, instinctive, animalistic ones based on your ego mind. If, however, you are able to create the space for your deepest wisdom, your heart, your love and compassion, even your forgiveness to be included, you can have a very different response. You may need to call 911 or you may need to sit with the person—holding them and allowing all of their emotion to pour out. Your deepest self, connected with ∞, will take charge and see the situation through to a course of action that is for everyone's highest good.

Fortunately, most of us will not have to face such a drastic situation, but if and when such a need arises, the more time you have spent mindfully, the more time you have meditated, the better equipped you will be to be *totally present* to the person who needs your help.

As I was instructed by my first teacher, we have opportunities throughout each and every day to practice being mindful. The following are some observations and thoughts about some of those everyday moments.

How often when you eat a meal do you really taste what you are eating? I mean really taste it. Usually, while interacting with others or thinking about completely different things, we put the food in our mouth, chew it a little, and then swallow. Our instinct and our animalistic hunger take over and we ingest the food as quick as we can. We want the calories. We need them for our physical energy, so we swallow them as soon as we've chewed enough to get the food down our throats. Yet, imagine what it would be like to go deeply into the flavor of the food.

Let's say it is a piece of chocolate—very fine Swiss chocolate imported from Europe. Most of the time, we eat it as if it were a candy bar from the grocery store. But what if we took the time to savor the chocolate? What flavors might we encounter? What might we observe about the consistency of the chocolate? Maybe we'd discover the creamy, smooth texture as it combines with our saliva, along with the sweet and salty taste created as they mix together. Imagine such an experience. If you took the time to enjoy that piece of chocolate and discover its many nuances, one piece eaten mindfully could fill you up more than gobbling down a whole chocolate bar.

How often when you eat a meal do you think about and appreciate where that food came from and how it was prepared? The next time you eat a salad, if you are able to eat it mindfully, I invite you to take in not only the taste of each fruit and vegetable, but to acknowledge how those fruits and vegetables came to exist on your plate. That salad offers you the chance to experience the energy of the earth going into your mouth. With each bite, you'll take in the energy of the person who watered the plants along with the energy of everyone who tended those plants from the time they were put in the ground to the time they were harvested. You'll ingest the energy of the sun, the rain, and all the nutrients that the soil provided. Imagine how different your experience of eating will be!

How often do you say things without thinking about your words before you speak them? Most of the time, people are not aware of what they say, at least not until they see the reaction to what they've said on the other person's face. At that moment, it's too late. We cannot take back our words once they've been spoken. So imagine cultivating a practice where you are able to say, "I am going to acknowledge what I say before it comes out of my mouth." Imagine not having to try and clean up the mess left by hurtful, critical, or judgmental words. Imagine not having to explain why you said what you said or having to apologize for the harm you've unintentionally caused. So much pain could be avoided for ourselves and others.

How often do we observe and appreciate the room in which we're sitting, even if it is a little messy or a bit crazy? Look around the room where you are right now as you're reading this. I imagine there are beautiful things that surround you. How often do you take the time to appreciate what is there rather than walk by those items without a single thought for them? Maybe the item that is sitting on your table was given to you as a thank you gift or to show you how much you are loved. Maybe you acquired the item that sits on your shelf while on a trip to another country. Maybe your child made it for you. Imagine taking the time to look at the item, to acknowledge it, to be grateful for it and for how it came to be in your life. Imagine being so thankful for what you have that you don't feel the need to acquire anything more. Imagine the sense of abundance you might feel as you really appreciate what you already have.

How often do you truly appreciate the people in your life, especially those you live with? Just like we do with the objects that surround us, we often take for granted the people who are in our lives every day. Whether at work or at home, we come to expect those people to be there. Imagine how it might be to acknowledge each person each day, maybe even multiple times a day. Imagine how it will feel for you and the other person when you let them know how much they mean to you, how much you appreciate them, and how grateful you are for their presence in your life. Imagine how enriched your relationships might be as a result of truly being present to them.

These are just a few examples, but they offer insights into what your life can be like when you are in total communion with every moment. When you are not hiding from anything, when you are not fighting or pushing or clinging or pulling, you allow love into your life. You allow peace and joy to exist. You allow deep wisdom and deep understanding to enter. You allow forgiveness, understanding, and compassion to move through you. You become a clear channel of ∞. You see things for what they are. You appreciate what is in your life at every moment with a deeper sense of what they are. When you begin to be present to everything in your life, your life becomes a living meditation.

THE RESPONSIBILITY OF MINDFULNESS

BEING MINDFUL OF WHERE you are at any given moment also means that you are aware of your own limitations, and this can make you stronger. For instance, I know that my body is not the same as it was when I was twenty. I am mindful of my age and my body. That means that I am mindful of how I move and what activities I engage in. I am mindful of what I carry and how I carry them. Being mindful of one's age is not a bad thing—there is actually a huge power in acknowledging exactly where you are. It may sound overly simple, but how often do you see people push themselves beyond their limits and then get hurt? By being mindful of exactly what I am capable of physically, I minimize the chances of getting injured. I also open myself to the full potential and possibilities of my age.

It's true, there are different experiences to be lived at different ages, and all of them are extremely important. We understand it when we see a baby stand up and take a few steps and then fall. We understand this primordial need for the baby to get up again and repeat the process over and over until the child begins to walk. Imagine the consequences if that one-year-old baby is denied the opportunity to walk. The consequences may not be as easy to see when a fifty-year-old or sixty-year-old denies their age and the experiences that accompany that stage of life, but just like the baby who doesn't learn to walk, there will be consequences. The possibilities and potential are mutated when we cannot respect exactly where we are in the present moment.

Whenever you deny or disregard the present moment, whenever you are not mindful, you risk things happening that you didn't want to occur. For instance, if you're running late for a meeting and you hurry, thinking about how late you're going to be, you might have an accident. Maybe you trip and fall as you are coming down the stairs. Not being mindful, you can do things like lose your keys. Because you weren't mindful at the time you set them down, you can end up searching your house, your car, your purse, and your pockets trying to locate them. As you set down the keys, you did not allow your mind to memorize your actions because you weren't even seeing what you were doing. If you were mindful, your memory will tell you exactly where they are. It is not because you have a bad memory, as I hear many people say. It is because you have a bad mindfulness practice.

It can also be because you expect that you can do multiple things at once, although your mind can only process one thing at a time. Acknowledging that limitation—that your mind can really only do one thing at a time—will not make you slower or stupid. It actually makes you more efficient and effective. The ego mind wants you to believe that this limitation is negative when in actuality acknowledging the need to finish one thing before you start something else is positive.

Multitasking can also be done through mental multitasking. I can be worrying about multiple things at the same time and they can prevent me from taking the steps that would serve me best in the moment. In the midst of a conversation with my spouse, I can be thinking about what I'll say next. If the mind only knows how to do one thing at a time, however, I need to understand that when I am talking or thinking I am not listening, and when I am listening I am not talking or thinking.

In our culture, we do not think that the mind can only do one thing at a time. I believe this is the reason that our hospitals are so full. Even when people drive, they listen to the radio while having a phone conversation; and those can both be happening while they're also trying to follow their GPS. Imagine the potential for a horrendous accident. How many people crash because they are doing multiple things while they are driving? Unfortunately, we normalize this behavior. We normalize and even encourage people to manage multiple tasks at one time. In the workplace, this can even be a requirement!

With mindfulness comes responsibility. If you ask me, "Why Felix do you think that people don't like to be mindful or to live mindfully?" my answer is, "Because if they are mindful, they have to be responsible!" Most people don't want to accept that level of responsibility. It's not only counter to what society normalizes, it means we have to look deeply into situations and circumstances in order to act consciously. Driving mindfully means we would do only one thing when we drive—drive—without allowing any other distractions to take us away from that one task. How many of us could drive that way?

Let me give another example related to the responsibility of mindfulness. The Fukushima nuclear disaster happened in 2011 and resulted in a meltdown of three of the plant's six nuclear reactors. Although people continue to act like nothing is happening, the radioactivity is continuing to do its job. The fish are becoming radioactive, but if you go to Japan you'll see that people are still eating sushi like nothing has changed. Their actions of "I don't want to be responsible" prevent them from acknowledging what has happened and what is continuing to happen. They are continuing to eat fish as if the fish is as good for them as it was before the disaster. Unfortunately, continuing to act from "I don't want to be responsible" is going to have further consequences—mostly to human beings. The earth will adapt and so will the plants and the sea life. But human beings will not be able to adapt to the radioactivity, and this will lead to illness, disease, and death.

In this example, the ego mind is not really mindful about what is happening. The ego mind is not able to decipher that something truly dangerous is happening. By not being mindful the ego mind becomes ignorant, and when it becomes ignorant it creates ignorant actions that create disaster—even destruction to itself.

When people start to become mindful something will need to change. Let's say a group of people create a one-hour primetime television program explaining what happened in 2011 and what is happening to Japan's fish supply as a result of those events. Let's say that by law everyone in Japan is required to watch the program and it awakens the Japanese people to the truth of the possibilities. Let's say all sorts of media get involved and there is ongoing mandatory emergency education that people must participate in. If the program and other media efforts make people aware of the dangers of continuing to eat raw fish, do you think the Japanese people will keep eating the fish as if nothing happened? I don't believe they will. I believe they'll realize that they have to change. In acknowledging the situation, the ego mind will not allow them to participate in and create a potential mass suicide. The ego mind is wired for survival, and it will not let itself die once it becomes aware of the entire situation.

The invitation is to become mindful and to accept responsibility in order that we can each awaken further to our full potential. If we acknowledge our responsibility, then we have to change. As soon as we say, "Yes, I am responsible and that is how it is," a new kind of action is required from each one of us. For those of us who accept that level of absolute responsibility, incredible magic happens.

CONCLUSION

THE INVITATION TO LIVE mindfully is always there. It is always waiting for us. To live in the present moment. To stay in the now. To be mindful in each and every moment. Yes, the invitation is always there. All we have to do is open ourselves to it and accept the invitation. Because we are human beings, though, this is both the easiest and most difficult responsibility to undertake.

There are two things in life that we know for sure will happen: change and death. That's it! And the ego doesn't like either one. The ego wants static and it wants to live forever. But those are impossible states to achieve. The ego dreams of finding a place where things don't change and where things are the way the ego wants. That's the spiritual search of most people: trying to find the place where they can do whatever they want and where everything will be okay—a place where nothing changes. So, most people's spiritual search is driven by their egos. That search can become a beautiful journey, though, because the ego follows pleasure, and like a mouse following the cheese, it gets trapped and must therefore undergo change. The biggest egos are often found in the spiritual world, because people need to get trapped in order to begin that inward journey. Ultimately, the ego has the opportunity to realize what is true—that there is no way for the ego to get closer to the spiritual truth without acknowledging its illusions.

Sometimes spiritual leaders use their egos as a tool to show others their truths. Being great spiritual teachers doesn't mean they will lose their ego and disappear in a cloud. The greatest teachers are going to use all of the tools that they have to invite others to see that what they have in their heads is illusion. A great teacher has to be human to be a true spiritual teacher.

The stories of Jesus, Buddha, and Mohammed are beautiful ones because these were human beings who showed us how to live both as people and as ∞. For our personal spiritual development, the humanity of these people is what is most significant and meaningful to us, not their ascensions. The spiritual illusion for many people, though, is that they focus on what is magic, which is neither real nor sustainable. The only thing we can actually do is realize our humanness and acknowledge the ∞ in us, just like Jesus, Buddha, and Mohammed did. Then, we put the ALL of what we are into manifestation. We are each ∞ and we are each human. As ∞, we can simultaneously see the desire and the ∞ within ourselves. That is the perfection of being human. That is our truth.

Most people believe that the opposite of love is hate. This is not true. The real truth is that the opposite of love is fear. And fear is a lack of faith. It is the inability to trust in ∞. If you are in fear a lot of the time, it means you distrust ∞. If you are rarely in fear, it means you have a lot of faith and are able to surrender to ∞. The invitation is always for us to move into love—for ourselves, for each other, and for ∞ within all of us.

Love leads us towards a *state of nothingness*. We are afraid of love because we are afraid of this nothingness—this blank canvas, this emptiness. We are afraid of the nothingness because it feels to the ego like we are dead, that we are nothing. The ego is something, so to the ego this "somethingness made into nothing" equals dying. And the ego *does not* want to die!

The main reason we have a limited relationship with spirituality is because we don't really want to jump into that *nothingness that is everything*. Once we do, we will become nothing. We will have no need for opinions because we will be nothing. Of course, the ego mind does not like this concept at all. How can we not have reactions, how can we not have goals, how can we not have expectations, how can we ignore our instincts? In this nothingness, we don't need any of these because we are and will be nothing.

Meditation is as difficult as it is for so many people, because we are afraid of this nothingness. We are afraid to enter this *state of nothing.* We want to be spiritual so we try to meditate, but the idea of touching the nothingness means to the ego that we will disappear. To satisfy the ego mind, we look for ways to meditate that still allow us to be with somethingness, which is why we use a mantra with our meditation or a rosary or mala.

Although the promise of nothingness is pure bliss, we continue to fight it. Our ego mind goes along with the beautiful experience of becoming more spiritual until the moment when it realizes there is nothing to get. Our ego minds have worked hard to develop our survival mechanisms, yet in this nothingness those survival mechanisms are not needed. The ego mind sees this as losing itself and disappearing, so it doesn't want to let go.

A heart that is strong and filled with love combined with a really powerful, strong ego represents a battle—it can create an explosion. We end up in the middle of that fight, and as a result it's only a matter of time for something really painful to happen. When there is no battle, there is no suffering. Ending the battle is ending the duality within our lives. When we stop the good versus bad, the ideas that someone is better than we are, that we need to compare ourselves to our neighbor, or compare the present to the past, then we can experience the present moment in all its perfection. Then we start to feel peaceful.

Our inner compass is always asking, "How am I feeling?" You can be uncomfortable and peaceful at the same time. So feeling uncomfortable is not a bad thing. You know you are in the hands of ∞ because you are peaceful, but you can be uncomfortable at the same time. "Go in peace," was Jesus's message. The more we can get comfortable with the discomfort and the peace, the more our egos can relax. Again, the invitation to trust in ∞ is always there.

The invitation to experience the nothingness is always present—it is always available to us. It is an invitation for each of us to awaken our curiosity so that it becomes stronger than the resistance of our ego mind. It is an invitation to grow the buffer within ourselves so that we have more space to experience more present moments and chose more conscious responses to situations. It is an invitation to remember each time we fully experience the present moment so that our heart muscle becomes stronger. Each time we enter the present moment fully, each time we enter the nothingness, we are living mindfully.

The promise of living mindfully is pure alchemy in that it transforms our ordinary lives into the magic of true joy and peace. It is complete love. It is total faith. It is pure tranquility. May you accept the invitation and become this nothingness that ∞ intended for you. May your mindfulness journey bring you home—to ∞ within. Namaste.

ACKNOWLEDGMENTS

SO MANY WONDERFUL PEOPLE have supported me through this journey of being a mindfulness/meditation teacher and in the process of writing this book.

I want to thank the people behind my work, those who believe in my contribution as a human. I especially thank those who don't understand or don't believe in my work and the way it is manifested, without whom this book would have been literally impossible. **Mettā** to you.

Thank you to all my teachers.

Thank you to ∞ for allowing me the opportunity to serve others and for the gift of the present moment, the only moment that is true.

Thank you to Donna Mazzitelli for bringing out the best of my thoughts into lucid expression.

Thank you to YOU, the reader, for giving yourself the chance to create a new way of possibilities in your life and in the life of others: "∞ possibilities."

And special thanks to the ones helping me alter the world to make it a less painful place. I really do appreciate you, and I thank ∞ for allowing me to share with you in this lifetime. I know you know who you guys are … **Mettā**

ABOUT THE AUTHOR

FELIX IS A SPIRITUAL leader dedicated to bringing people throughout the world a practical path of healing, mindfulness and meditation in an accessible way. Drawing on his path as a former Buddhist monk, Energy Healer, and as an artist, Felix offers a unique perspective on mindfulness and the present moment.

Each present moment is filled with gifts. When all focus and energy is in the present moment, we are open to receive each gift as a true present. This is the real present of being present—to be in touch with the only thing that is real, The Now.

With his first book, *Mindfulness: The Alchemy of Now,* Felix's intention is to diminish the amount of distortion—suffering— that is created by visiting the time zones of the past and the future, and invites people to fully experience "The Now" to receive the true gifts of the present moment.

To learn more about Felix and his work, please visit www.FelixLopez.org.

ABOUT THE PRESS

Merry Dissonance Press is a book producer/indie publisher of works of transformation, inspiration, exploration, and illumination. MDP takes a holistic approach to bringing books into the world that make a little noise and create dissonance within the whole in order that ALL can be resolved to produce beautiful harmonies.

Merry Dissonance Press works with its authors every step of the way to craft the finest books and help promote them. Dedicated to publishing award-winning books, we strive to support talented writers and assist them to discover, claim, and refine their own distinct voice. **Merry Dissonance Press** is the place where collaboration and facilitation of our shared human experiences join together to make a difference in our world.

Visit http://merrydissonancepress.com/ for more information.

tional instruction that builds to chapters on forgiveness, developing compassion, cultivating inner peace, and accepting personal responsibility for our own joy and that of others.

In *Mindfulness*, Lopez set out to create a recipe for a rich and flavorful life. It's a culmination of all the self-care and spiritual teachings of the past, simply explained and tied together with language that is beautifully poetic at times. As such, it may be the last book his audience of seekers will ever need, containing enough wisdom to last a lifetime."

—Starred Review, BlueInk Review